Taste of H...
Slow Cooker

TASTE OF HOME BOOKS • RDA ENTHUSIAST BRANDS, LLC • MILWAUKEE, WI

Taste of Home

GET SOCIAL WITH US

To find a recipe tasteofhome.com
To submit a recipe tasteofhome.com/submit
To find out about other *Taste of Home* products shoptasteofhome.co

LIKE US
facebook.com/tasteofhome

PIN US
pinterest.com/taste_of_home

FOLLOW US
@tasteofhome

TWEET US
twitter.com/tasteofhome

TABLE OF CONTENTS

Sausage with Jalapeno Potatoes, page 160
Peachy Baby Back Ribs, page 135

There's Always Time for
Home Cooking!

Everyone is busy these days—adults who work long hours, kids who have full schedules of after-school activities—and home-cooked meals too often fall by the wayside. But in this era of constant time crunches, the slow cooker has become a go-to kitchen tool that brings home-cooked food back to the tables of even the busiest cooks.

It's all about flexibility. By using a slow cooker, you can do prep work on your own schedule and eat when you're ready. Load the cooker in the morning; a delicious, hot meal will be ready to serve when you get home. Slow cookers also free up oven and stovetop space when you're fixing multi-course meals, and enable you to carry dishes along to an office party or keep a tasty treat warm on a weekend buffet.

Taste of Home Slow Cooker includes 100 recipes that let you take advantage of the possibilities—whether you're making main courses, side dishes, even desserts! Throughout, you'll find tips that will help you make the most of your slow cooker and achieve the depth of flavor that slow cooking brings out.

HOW TO KEEP YOUR COOKER CLEAN

- Allow the stoneware insert to cool before rinsing it. Wash it in the dishwasher or sink with warm, soapy water.
- Do not use abrasive cleansers.
- Use a damp sponge to clean the metal base. Do not soak the base in water.
- To remove white mineral stains from the insert, fill the cooker with hot water mixed with 1 cup of white vinegar and heat on high for two hours. Empty the insert, let it cool, and wash as usual.

Try this
Zesty Italian Beef Sandwich,
page 16.

Slow Cooker Pizza Casserole, page 56

Molten Mocha Cake, page 202

10 TOP TIPS FOR SLOW COOKING

CHOOSE THE RIGHT CUT OF MEAT. Lower-prestige (and lower-cost!) cuts work better than leaner cuts. Fat breaks down during the cooking process, so the marbling inside the meat will result in a dish that melts in your mouth. Go for dark meat when cooking poultry.

DON'T PEEK! Each time you open the cooker, you'll need to add 15-20 minutes of cooking time. Unless the recipe calls for adding ingredients during the cooking process—hands off!

AVOID TEMPERATURE SHOCKS. If you're using a cooker with a ceramic insert, avoid any sudden temperature changes. Put a dish towel on a cold work surface before setting the hot insert down. Don't transfer an insert from the refrigerator to a preheated base; start with an unheated base, or let the insert come to room temperature first.

THAW THE FROZEN BITS. Thaw frozen food before adding it to the slow cooker (unless the recipe specifies otherwise). Frozen ingredients lower temperatures inside the cooker and increase the chance of bacteria growing.

DON'T OVERFILL IT. Fill the slow cooker between one-half and two-thirds full.

GO EASY ON THE ALCOHOL. Alcohol won't evaporate, so use it sparingly or go for a nonalcoholic option. If you brown the meat, use wine to deglaze the pan, then pour the liquid into the slow cooker. This technique will burn off the alcohol but leave the flavor.

ADD DAIRY LATE. Dairy breaks down, or separates, in a slow cooker, so add yogurt or sour cream in the final mix stage, just before serving.

USE LESS LIQUID. Liquids given up by the ingredients will remain in the pot instead of evaporating. That's why many recipes call for condensed soup instead of liquid broth or stock. When adapting a traditional recipe for your slow cooker, reduce the liquid by a third.

DON'T LET IT GET COLD. If you won't be home when the cooking time is up, be sure the cooker will switch itself to Warm. Temperatures between 40-140° are where bacteria thrive.

HALVE THE TIME BY DOUBLING THE SETTING. On most models, Low is 170° and High is 280°. Cooking on low takes twice as long as cooking on high. For many (not all) recipes, cranking up the heat will cut down the cook time.

SOUPS, SIDES &
SANDWICHES

SO-SIMPLE MINESTRONE

Even the die-hard meat lovers in your family won't be able to get enough of this savory meatless soup. If you prefer a thicker consistency, mash half of the garbanzo beans before adding them to the slow cooker.

—PAULA ZSIRAY LOGAN, UT

PREP: 10 MIN. • **COOK:** 8½ HOURS
MAKES: 12 SERVINGS (ABOUT 3 QUARTS)

- 2 **cans (14½ ounces each) chicken or vegetable broth**
- 1 **can (28 ounces) crushed tomatoes**
- 1 **can (16 ounces) kidney beans, rinsed and drained**
- 1 **can (15 ounces) garbanzo beans or chickpeas, rinsed and drained**
- 1 **can (14½ ounces) beef broth**
- 2 **cups frozen cubed hash brown potatoes, thawed**
- 1 **tablespoon dried minced onion**
- 1 **tablespoon dried parsley flakes**
- 1 **teaspoon salt**
- 1 **teaspoon dried oregano**
- ½ **teaspoon garlic powder**
- ½ **teaspoon dried basil**
- ½ **teaspoon dried marjoram**
- 1 **package (10 ounces) frozen chopped spinach, thawed and drained**
- 2 **cups frozen peas and carrots, thawed**

In a 5-qt. slow cooker, combine the first 13 ingredients. Cover and cook on low for 8 hours. Stir in spinach and peas and carrots; cook 30 minutes longer or until heated through.

CHILI CONEY DOGS

PREP: 20 MIN. • **COOK:** 4 HOURS • **MAKES:** 8 SERVINGS

- 1 **pound lean ground beef (90% lean)**
- 1 **can (15 ounces) tomato sauce**
- ½ **cup water**
- 2 **tablespoons Worcestershire sauce**
- 1 **tablespoon dried minced onion**
- ½ **teaspoon garlic powder**
- ½ **teaspoon ground mustard**
- ½ **teaspoon chili powder**
- ½ **teaspoon pepper**
  Dash cayenne pepper
- 8 **hot dogs**
- 8 **hot dog buns, split**
  Optional toppings: shredded cheddar cheese, relish and chopped onion

1. In a large skillet, cook beef over medium heat for 6-8 minutes or until meat is no longer pink, breaking into crumbles; drain. Stir in tomato sauce, water, Worcestershire sauce, onion and seasonings.

2. Place hot dogs in a 3-qt. slow cooker; top with the beef mixture. Cook, covered, on low for 4-5 hours or until heated through. Serve on buns with toppings as desired.

Everyone in our family, from the smallest kid to the oldest adult, loves these dogs. They're so easy to throw together and heat up in the slow cooker.

—**MICHELE HARRIS** VICKSBURG, MI

CAROLINA-STYLE PORK BARBECUE

I am originally from North Carolina and this recipe for the slow cooker is one my family adores. My husband swears my authentic Carolina 'cue is the best BBQ he has ever eaten!
—KATHRYN RANSOM WILLIAMS SPARKS, NV

PREP: 30 MIN. • **COOK:** 6 HOURS • **MAKES:** 14 SERVINGS

- 1 boneless pork shoulder butt roast (4 to 5 pounds)
- 2 tablespoons brown sugar
- 2 teaspoons salt
- 1 teaspoon paprika
- ½ teaspoon pepper
- 2 medium onions, quartered
- ¾ cup cider vinegar
- 4 teaspoons Worcestershire sauce
- 1 tablespoon sugar
- 1 tablespoon crushed red pepper flakes
- 1 teaspoon garlic salt
- 1 teaspoon ground mustard
- ½ teaspoon cayenne pepper
- 14 hamburger buns, split
- 1¾ pounds deli coleslaw

1. Cut roast into quarters. Mix brown sugar, salt, paprika and pepper; rub over meat. Place the meat and onions in a 5-qt. slow cooker.

2. In a small bowl, whisk vinegar, Worcestershire sauce, sugar and seasonings; pour over roast. Cook, covered, on low for 6-8 hours or until the meat is tender.

3. Remove roast; cool slightly. Reserve 1½ cups cooking juices; discard remaining juices. Skim fat from the reserved juices. Shred the meat with two forks. Return the shredded pork and reserved juices to slow cooker; heat through. Serve on buns with coleslaw.

NOTE *You can also reheat the pork in a saucepan over a campfire or a portable cook stove.*

SLOW COOKER LASAGNA SOUP

Try this soup if you're looking for a distinctive—and healthier—take on traditional lasagna.

—SHARON GERST NORTH LIBERTY, IA

PREP: 35 MIN. • **COOK:** 5 HOURS + STANDING
MAKES: 8 SERVINGS (2½ QUARTS)

- 1½ pounds bulk Italian sausage
- 1 large onion, chopped
- 2 medium carrots, chopped
- 2 cups sliced fresh mushrooms
- 3 garlic cloves, minced
- 1 carton (32 ounces) chicken broth
- 2 cans (14½ ounces each) Italian stewed tomatoes
- 1 can (15 ounces) tomato sauce
- 6 lasagna noodles, broken into 1-inch pieces
- 2 cups coarsely chopped fresh spinach
- 1 cup cubed or shredded part-skim mozzarella cheese
- ½ cup shredded Parmesan cheese
  Thinly sliced fresh basil, optional

1. In a large skillet, cook sausage over medium-high heat for 8-10 minutes or until no longer pink, breaking into crumbles; drain. Transfer to a 5- or 6-qt. slow cooker.

2. Add onion and carrots to the same skillet; cook and stir for 2-4 minutes or until the vegetables are softened. Stir in mushrooms and garlic; cook and stir for 2-4 minutes or until the mushrooms are softened. Transfer to slow cooker. Stir in broth, tomatoes and tomato sauce. Cook, covered, on low for 4-6 hours or until vegetables are tender.

3. Skim fat from soup. Add lasagna noodles; cook 1 hour longer or until the noodles are tender. Stir in spinach. Remove the slow cooker insert; let stand for 10 minutes. Divide mozzarella cheese among individual serving bowls; ladle soup over the cheese. Sprinkle with Parmesan cheese and, if desired, basil.

BROCCOLI & CHEESE

This crumb-topped side dish is quick to assemble and full of flavor. Since it simmers in a slow cooker, it frees up my oven for other things, which is a great help when I'm preparing several items for a big meal.
—CONNIE SLOCUM ANTIOCH, TN

PREP: 10 MIN. • **COOK:** 2¾ HOURS • **MAKES:** 10 SERVINGS

- 6 **cups frozen chopped broccoli, partially thawed**
- 1 **can (10¾ ounces) condensed cream of celery soup, undiluted**
- 1½ **cups shredded sharp cheddar cheese, divided**
- ¼ **cup chopped onion**
- ½ **teaspoon Worcestershire sauce**
- ¼ **teaspoon pepper**
- 1 **cup crushed butter-flavored crackers (about 25)**
- 2 **tablespoons butter**

1. In a large bowl, combine broccoli, soup, 1 cup of cheese, onion, Worcestershire sauce and pepper. Pour into a greased 3-qt. slow cooker. Sprinkle crackers on top; dot with butter.
2. Cover and cook on high for 2½-3 hours. Sprinkle with the remaining cheese. Cook for 10 minutes longer or until the cheese is melted.

NOTES

ZESTY ITALIAN BEEF SANDWICHES

It's so easy to build a zesty sandwich when you pile on shredded, spiced beef, pickles and smoked provolone. Can't find smoked provolone? Regular works, too!

—CRYSTAL SCHLUETER NORTHGLENN, CO

PREP: 15 MIN. • **COOK:** 8 HOURS • **MAKES:** 6 SERVINGS

- 1 **boneless beef chuck roast (3 to 4 pounds)**
- 1 **can (10½ ounces) condensed French onion soup, undiluted**
- ½ **cup cider vinegar**
- 2 **tablespoons reduced-sodium soy sauce**
- 1 **tablespoon brown sugar**
- ½ **cup mayonnaise**
- 1 **tablespoon horseradish mustard or spicy brown mustard**
- 1 **tablespoon chili garlic sauce**
- 6 **Italian rolls, split**
- 6 **thin slices red onion**
- 18 **sweet pickle slices**
- 6 **slices smoked provolone cheese**
   Lettuce leaves, optional

1. Place chuck roast in a 5- or 6-qt. slow cooker. In a small bowl, mix soup, vinegar, soy sauce and brown sugar; pour over the roast. Cook, covered, on low 8-10 hours or until the meat is tender.

2. Remove roast; cool slightly. Shred meat with two forks. Return shredded meat to the slow cooker; heat through. In a small bowl, mix mayonnaise, mustard and chili sauce; spread on roll bottoms. Layer with onion, pickles, shredded beef, cheese and lettuce. Replace roll tops.

HELPFUL HINT

You can swap dried beans for canned in this recipe, but remember that dried beans still need to be fully soaked—slow cooking is not a substitute for soaking.

TEX-MEX CHILI

Hearty and spicy, this is a stick-to-your-ribs chili for sure. You can also simmer it on the stovetop—the longer you cook it, the better.
—ERIC HAYES ANTIOCH, CA

PREP: 20 MIN. • **COOK:** 6 HOURS
MAKES: 12 SERVINGS (1⅓ CUPS EACH)

- 3 **pounds beef stew meat**
- 1 **tablespoon canola oil**
- 3 **garlic cloves, minced**
- 3 **cans (16 ounces each) kidney beans, rinsed and drained**
- 3 **cans (15 ounces each) tomato sauce**
- 1 **can (14½ ounces) diced tomatoes, undrained**
- 1 **cup water**
- 1 **can (6 ounces) tomato paste**
- ¾ **cup salsa verde**
- 1 **envelope chili seasoning**
- 2 **teaspoons dried minced onion**
- 1 **teaspoon chili powder**
- ½ **teaspoon crushed red pepper flakes**
- ½ **teaspoon ground cumin**
- ½ **teaspoon cayenne pepper**
  Shredded cheddar cheese and minced fresh cilantro

1. In a large skillet, brown stew meat in oil in batches. Add garlic; cook 1 minute longer. Transfer to a 6-qt. slow cooker.
2. Stir in beans, tomato sauce, tomatoes, water, tomato paste, salsa verde and seasonings. Cover and cook on low for 6-8 hours or until the meat is tender. Garnish individual servings with cheese and cilantro.
FREEZE OPTION *Before adding toppings, cool the chili. Freeze chili in freezer containers. To use, partially thaw in refrigerator overnight. Heat through in a saucepan, stirring occasionally and adding a little broth or water if necessary. Sprinkle each serving with cheese and cilantro.*

HEARTY HOMEMADE CHICKEN NOODLE SOUP

This satisfying homemade soup with a hint of cayenne is brimming with vegetables, chicken and noodles. The recipe came from my father-in-law, but I made some adjustments to give it my own spin.
—NORMA REYNOLDS OVERLAND PARK, KS

PREP: 20 MIN. • **COOK:** 5½ HOURS
MAKES: 12 SERVINGS (3 QUARTS)

- 12 **fresh baby carrots, cut into ½-inch pieces**
- 4 **celery ribs, cut into ½-inch pieces**
- ¾ **cup finely chopped onion**
- 1 **tablespoon minced fresh parsley**
- ½ **teaspoon pepper**
- ¼ **teaspoon cayenne pepper**
- 1½ **teaspoons mustard seed**
- 2 **garlic cloves, peeled and halved**
- 1¼ **pounds boneless skinless chicken breast halves**
- 1¼ **pounds boneless skinless chicken thighs**
- 4 **cans (14½ ounces each) chicken broth**
- 1 **package (9 ounces) refrigerated linguine**

1. In a 5-qt. slow cooker, combine the first six ingredients. Place mustard seed and garlic on a double thickness of cheesecloth; bring up corners of cloth and tie with kitchen string to form a bag. Place in the slow cooker. Add chicken and broth. Cover and cook on low for 5-6 hours or until the meat is tender.

2. Discard the spice bag. Remove the chicken; let it cool slightly. Stir linguine into soup; cover and cook on high for 30 minutes or until tender. Cut the chicken into pieces and return to the soup; heat through.

FRENCH DIP

PREP: 15 MIN. • **COOK:** 5 HOURS • **MAKES:** 8 SERVINGS

- 1 **beef chuck roast (3 pounds), trimmed**
- 2 **cups water**
- ½ **cup reduced-sodium soy sauce**
- 1 **teaspoon dried rosemary, crushed**
- 1 **teaspoon dried thyme**
- 1 **teaspoon garlic powder**
- 1 **bay leaf**
- 3 **to 4 whole peppercorns**
- 8 **French rolls, split**

1. Place roast in a 5-qt. slow cooker. Add water, soy sauce and seasonings. Cover and cook on high for 5-6 hours or until the beef is tender.

2. Remove the roast from the broth; shred the meat with two forks and keep warm. Strain broth; skim fat. Pour the broth into small cups. Serve the beef on rolls; use the cups of broth for dipping.

For a sandwich with more pizzazz than the traditional French dip, give this recipe a try. The seasonings give the broth a wonderful flavor, and the meat cooks up tender and juicy. This version will soon be a favorite at your house, too.

—MARGARET MCNEIL GERMANTOWN, TN

RANCH POTATOES

Even after seven years, my family still asks for this tasty potato and bacon dish. Try it once and I bet your family will be hooked, too.
—LYNN IRELAND LEBANON, WI

PREP: 15 MIN. • **COOK:** 7 HOURS
MAKES: 10 SERVINGS

- **6 bacon strips, chopped**
- **2½ pounds small red potatoes, cubed**
- **1 package (8 ounces) cream cheese, softened**
- **1 can (10¾ ounces) condensed cream of potato soup, undiluted**
- **¼ cup 2% milk**
- **1 envelope buttermilk ranch salad dressing mix**
- **3 tablespoons thinly sliced green onions**

1. In a large skillet, cook bacon over medium heat until crisp, stirring occasionally. Remove with a slotted spoon; drain on paper towels. Drain drippings, reserving 1 tablespoon.

2. Place potatoes in a 3-qt. slow cooker. In a bowl, beat cream cheese, soup, milk, dressing mix and the reserved drippings until blended; stir into the potatoes. Sprinkle with the bacon.

3. Cook, covered, on low for 7-8 hours or until the potatoes are tender. Top with green onions.

CHEDDAR-FONTINA MAC & CHEESE

My sons say that I am the best mom in the world whenever I make this creamy mac and cheese perfection. You can't beat a response like that!

—HEIDI FLEEK HAMBURG, PA

PREP: 25 MIN. • **COOK:** 1 HOUR • **MAKES:** 8 SERVINGS

- 2 **cups uncooked elbow macaroni**
- 1 **can (10¾ ounces) condensed cheddar cheese soup, undiluted**
- 1 **cup 2% milk**
- ½ **cup sour cream**
- ¼ **cup butter, cubed**
- ½ **teaspoon onion powder**
- ¼ **teaspoon white pepper**
- ⅛ **teaspoon salt**
- 1 **cup shredded cheddar cheese**
- 1 **cup shredded fontina cheese**
- 1 **cup shredded provolone cheese**

1. Cook macaroni according to package directions for al dente. Meanwhile, in a large saucepan, combine soup, milk, sour cream, butter and seasonings; cook and stir over medium-low heat until blended. Stir in cheeses until melted.
2. Drain the macaroni; transfer to a greased 3-qt. slow cooker. Stir in the cheese mixture. Cook, covered, on low for 1-2 hours or until heated through.

TRADITIONAL STUFFING

PREP: 30 MIN. • **COOK:** 3 HOURS • **MAKES:** 10 SERVINGS

- 1 **cup chopped onion**
- 1 **cup chopped celery**
- ¼ **cup butter**
- 6 **cups cubed day-old white bread**
- 6 **cups cubed day-old whole wheat bread**
- 1 **teaspoon salt**
- 1 **teaspoon poultry seasoning**
- 1 **teaspoon rubbed sage**
- ½ **teaspoon pepper**
- 1 **can (14½ ounces) reduced-sodium chicken broth or vegetable broth**
- 2 **large eggs, beaten**

1. In a small nonstick skillet over medium heat, cook onion and celery in butter until tender.

2. In a large bowl, combine bread cubes, salt, poultry seasoning, sage and pepper. Stir in the onion mixture. Combine the broth and eggs; add to the bread mixture and toss to coat.

3. Transfer to a 3-qt. slow cooker coated with cooking spray. Cover and cook on low for 3-4 hours or until a thermometer reads 160°.

If you're hosting a big Thanksgiving dinner this year, add this simple slow-cooked stuffing to your menu to ease entertaining. The recipe comes in handy when you run out of oven space at large family gatherings.

—DONALD SEILER MACON, MS

WHITE BEAN CHICKEN CHILI

My sister shared this chili recipe with me, but I usually double it and add an extra can of beans. The jalapeno adds just enough heat to notice but not too much for my children.

—KRISTINE BOWLES RIO RANCHO, NM

PREP: 25 MIN. • **COOK:** 3 HOURS
MAKES: 6 SERVINGS

- ¾ **pound boneless skinless chicken breasts, cut into 1¼-inch pieces**
- ¼ **teaspoon salt**
- ¼ **teaspoon pepper**
- 2 **tablespoons olive oil, divided**
- 1 **medium onion, chopped**
- 1 **jalapeno pepper, seeded and chopped**
- 4 **garlic cloves, minced**
- 2 **teaspoons dried oregano**
- 1 **teaspoon ground cumin**
- 2 **cans (15 ounces each) white kidney or cannellini beans, rinsed and drained, divided**
- 2½ **cups chicken broth, divided**
- 1½ **cups shredded cheddar cheese**
  Optional toppings: sliced avocado, quartered cherry tomatoes and chopped cilantro

1. Toss chicken with salt and pepper. In a large skillet, heat 1 tablespoon oil over medium-high heat; saute the chicken until browned. Transfer to a 3-qt. slow cooker.

2. In the same skillet, heat remaining oil over medium heat; saute onion until tender. Add jalapeno, garlic, oregano and cumin; cook and stir for 2 minutes. Add to slow cooker.

3. In a bowl, mash 1 cup of the beans; stir in ½ cup broth. Stir bean mixture and the remaining whole beans and broth into the chicken mixture.

4. Cook, covered, on low until the chicken is tender, 3-3½ hours. Stir before serving. Serve with cheese and top as desired.

FREEZE OPTION *Freeze cooled chili in freezer containers. To use, partially thaw in refrigerator overnight. Heat through in a saucepan, stirring occasionally and adding a little broth or water if necessary.*

CHICKEN CORN CHILI *Add 2 cups thawed frozen corn and ½ teaspoon ground coriander to slow cooker along with broth. Proceed as directed.*

NOTE *Wear disposable gloves when cutting hot peppers; the oils can burn skin. Avoid touching your face.*

ROOT BEER PULLED PORK SANDWICHES

My husband is a huge fan of pulled pork sandwiches, so my sister shared this incredibly easy recipe with me. At potlucks and family dinners, nobody can get enough of this root beer-braised version.
—CAROLYN PALM WALTON, NY

PREP: 20 MIN. • **COOK:** 8½ HOURS • **MAKES:** 12 SERVINGS

- 1 **boneless pork shoulder butt roast (3 to 4 pounds)**
- 1 **can (12 ounces) root beer or cola**
- 1 **bottle (18 ounces) barbecue sauce**
- 12 **kaiser rolls, split**

1. Place roast in a 4- or 5-qt. slow cooker. Add root beer; cook, covered, on low for 8-10 hours or until meat is tender.
2. Remove roast; cool slightly. Discard cooking juices. Shred pork with two forks; return meat to slow cooker. Stir in barbecue sauce. Cook, covered, until heated through, about 30 minutes. Serve on rolls.

FREEZE OPTION *Freeze cooled meat mixture in freezer containers. To use, partially thaw in refrigerator overnight. Heat through in a saucepan, stirring occasionally and adding a little water if necessary.*

NOTES

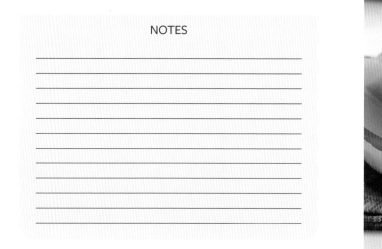

SLOW-COOKED BEAN MEDLEY

I often change the variety of beans in this classic recipe, using whatever I have on hand to total five 15- to 16-ounce cans. The sauce makes any combination delicious! It's a gluten-free side dish that's popular with everyone.
—**PEGGY GWILLIM** STRASBOURG, SK

PREP: 25 MIN. • **COOK:** 5 HOURS
MAKES: 12 SERVINGS (¾ CUP EACH)

- 1½ **cups ketchup**
- 2 **celery ribs, chopped**
- 1 **medium onion, chopped**
- 1 **medium green pepper, chopped**
- 1 **medium sweet red pepper, chopped**
- ½ **cup packed brown sugar**
- ½ **cup water**
- ½ **cup Italian salad dressing**
- 2 **bay leaves**
- 1 **tablespoon cider vinegar**
- 1 **teaspoon ground mustard**
- ⅛ **teaspoon pepper**
- 1 **can (16 ounces) kidney beans, rinsed and drained**
- 1 **can (15½ ounces) black-eyed peas, rinsed and drained**
- 1 **can (15½ ounces) great northern beans, rinsed and drained**
- 1 **can (15¼ ounces) whole kernel corn, drained**
- 1 **can (15¼ ounces) lima beans, rinsed and drained**
- 1 **can (15 ounces) black beans, rinsed and drained**

In a 5-qt. slow cooker, combine the first 12 ingredients. Stir in the remaining ingredients. Cover and cook on low for 5-6 hours or until the onion and peppers are tender. Discard the bay leaves before serving.

ITALIAN MEATBALL SUBS

A flavorful tomato sauce and mildly spiced meatballs make a hearty sandwich filling—or they can be served over pasta. I broil the meatballs first to quickly brown them.

—JEAN GLACKEN ELKTON, MD

PREP: 25 MIN. • **COOK:** 4 HOURS • **MAKES:** 6-7 SERVINGS

- **2 large eggs, lightly beaten**
- **¼ cup milk**
- **½ cup dry bread crumbs**
- **2 tablespoons grated Parmesan cheese**
- **1 teaspoon salt**
- **¼ teaspoon pepper**
- **⅛ teaspoon garlic powder**
- **1 pound ground beef**
- **½ pound bulk Italian sausage**

SAUCE

- **1 can (15 ounces) tomato sauce**
- **1 can (6 ounces) tomato paste**
- **1 small onion, chopped**
- **½ cup chopped green pepper**
- **½ cup dry red wine or beef broth**
- **⅓ cup water**
- **2 garlic cloves, minced**
- **1 teaspoon dried oregano**
- **1 teaspoon salt**
- **½ teaspoon sugar**
- **½ teaspoon pepper**
- **6 to 7 Italian rolls, split**
  Shredded Parmesan cheese, optional

1. In a large bowl, combine eggs and milk; add bread crumbs, cheese, salt, pepper and garlic powder. Add beef and sausage; mix well. Shape into 1-in. balls. Preheat broiler. Place meatballs in a 15x10x1-in. baking pan. Broil 4 in. from the heat for 4 minutes; turn and broil 3 minutes longer.

2. Transfer to a 5-qt. slow cooker. Combine tomato sauce and paste, onion, green pepper, wine, water and seasonings; pour over the meatballs. Cover and cook on low for 4-5 hours. Serve on rolls. Sprinkle with shredded cheese if desired.

SLOW-COOKED SPLIT PEA SOUP

PREP: 15 MIN. • **COOK:** 7 HOURS
MAKES: 8 SERVINGS (ABOUT 3 QUARTS)

- 1 **meaty ham bone or 2 pounds smoked ham hocks**
- 1 **package (16 ounces) dried green split peas**
- 1 **pound potatoes, peeled and cubed (about 3 cups)**
- 1 **large onion, chopped**
- 2 **medium carrots, chopped**
- 1 **tablespoon dried celery flakes**
- ½ **teaspoon garlic powder**
- ½ **teaspoon dried thyme**
- ½ **teaspoon dried basil**
- ¼ **teaspoon lemon-pepper seasoning**
- ⅛ **teaspoon dried marjoram**
- 1 **bay leaf**
- 6 **cups reduced-sodium chicken broth**

1. In a 4- or 5-qt. slow cooker, combine all ingredients. Cook, covered, on low for 7-9 hours or until the split peas are tender.
2. Remove ham bone from soup. When cool enough to handle, remove meat from bone; discard bone. Cut the meat into cubes and return to soup or save for another use. Remove the bay leaf before serving.
FREEZE OPTION *Freeze cooled soup in freezer containers. To use, partially thaw in refrigerator overnight. Heat through in a saucepan, stirring occasionally and adding a little broth if necessary.*

> I've been making this soup for years.
> After every holiday when ham is served,
> the hostess sends me home with the
> ham bone and a bag of split peas so I can
> cook up this family favorite.
>
> —SUSAN SIMONS EATONVILLE, WA

SLOW-COOKED BARBECUED BEEF SANDWICHES

After simmering in a rich homemade sauce all day, chuck roast makes delicious shredded beef sandwiches.

—**TATINA SMITH** SAN ANGELO, TX

PREP: 20 MIN. • **COOK:** 8¼ HOURS
MAKES: 12 SERVINGS

- 1 **boneless beef chuck roast (3 pounds)**
- 1½ **cups ketchup**
- ¼ **cup packed brown sugar**
- ¼ **cup barbecue sauce**
- 2 **tablespoons Worcestershire sauce**
- 2 **tablespoons Dijon mustard**
- 1 **teaspoon liquid smoke, optional**
- ½ **teaspoon salt**
- ¼ **teaspoon garlic powder**
- ¼ **teaspoon pepper**
- 12 **sandwich buns, split**
   Sliced onions, dill pickles and pickled jalapenos, optional

1. Cut roast in half and place in a 3- or 4-qt. slow cooker. Combine ketchup, brown sugar, barbecue sauce, Worcestershire sauce, mustard, liquid smoke if desired and seasonings. Pour over the beef.
2. Cover and cook on low for 8-10 hours or until the meat is tender. Remove the meat; cool slightly. Skim fat from the cooking liquid.
3. Shred beef with two forks; return to the slow cooker. Cover and cook for 15 minutes or until heated through.

Using a slotted spoon, place ½ cup on each bun. Serve with onions, pickles and jalapenos if desired.

FREEZE OPTION *Place individual portions of cooled meat mixture in freezer containers. To use, partially thaw in refrigerator overnight. Microwave, covered, on high until heated through, gently stirring; add broth or water if necessary.*

TEX-MEX BEEF SANDWICHES *Omit ketchup, brown sugar, barbecue sauce, Worcestershire sauce, mustard, liquid smoke, salt, garlic powder, pepper and optional toppings. Combine 1 envelope burrito seasoning with 2 tablespoons baking cocoa; rub over beef. Place 1 each coarsely chopped sweet red pepper, green pepper and large onion in slow cooker; top with meat. Combine 1 cup beef broth with ½ cup ketchup. Pour over meat; proceed as recipe directs.*

BARBECUED VENISON SANDWICHES *Substitute one 3- to 4-pound boneless venison roast for the beef.*

ITALIAN BEEF SANDWICHES *Omit ketchup, brown sugar, barbecue sauce, Worcestershire sauce, mustard, liquid smoke, salt, garlic powder, pepper and optional toppings. Sprinkle roast with 1 teaspoon of Italian seasoning and ¼ teaspoon each cayenne and black pepper. Place in slow cooker. Combine ¼ cup water, 1 jar (16 oz.) pepperoncini with liquid, 1 each julienned sweet red pepper and green pepper, 1 minced garlic clove, 1 envelope onion soup mix and 2 tablespoons Worcestershire sauce. Pour over meat; proceed as recipe directs.*

AUTUMN PUMPKIN CHILI

I've prepared this chili often and everyone seems to love it, even the most finicky grandchildren. It's also earned thumbs-up with family and friends in other states. It's a definite keeper in my book!
—KIMBERLY NAGY PORT HADLOCK, WA

PREP: 20 MIN. • **COOK:** 7 HOURS • **MAKES:** 4 SERVINGS

- 1 **medium onion, chopped**
- 1 **small green pepper, chopped**
- 1 **small sweet yellow pepper, chopped**
- 1 **tablespoon canola oil**
- 1 **garlic clove, minced**
- 1 **pound ground turkey**
- 1 **can (15 ounces) solid-pack pumpkin**
- 1 **can (14½ ounces) diced tomatoes, undrained**
- 4½ **teaspoons chili powder**
- ¼ **teaspoon pepper**
- ¼ **teaspoon salt**
  Optional toppings: shredded cheddar cheese, sour cream and sliced green onions

1. In a large skillet, saute onion and green and yellow peppers in oil until tender. Add garlic; cook 1 minute longer. Crumble turkey into skillet. Cook over medium heat until the meat is no longer pink.

2. Transfer to a 3-qt. slow cooker. Stir in pumpkin, tomatoes, chili powder, pepper and salt. Cover and cook on low for 7-9 hours. Serve with toppings of your choice.

NOTES

SWEET & SPICY PULLED PORK SANDWICHES

I threw some always-available condiments into my slow cooker with a pork roast to create this fantastic pulled pork. It has become a staple sandwich filler for large get-togethers. Serve with rolls, on top of toasted crostini, or as a filling for empanadas. The flavor of the pork goes well with a glass of white wine.

—LORI TERRY CHICAGO, IL

PREP: 30 MIN. • **COOK:** 8 HOURS • **MAKES:** 10 SERVINGS

- 2 **medium onions, sliced (about 2 cups)**
- 2 **tablespoons brown sugar**
- 1 **tablespoon smoked paprika**
- 1½ **teaspoons salt**
- ½ **teaspoon pepper**
- 1 **boneless pork shoulder roast (4 to 5 pounds)**
- ½ **cup chicken or vegetable broth**
- ¼ **cup cider vinegar**
- 3 **tablespoons reduced-sodium soy sauce**
- 3 **tablespoons Worcestershire sauce**
- 2 **tablespoons Sriracha Asian hot chili sauce**
- 1 **tablespoon molasses**
- 2 **garlic cloves, minced**
- 2 **teaspoons Dijon mustard**
- 3 **cups coleslaw mix**
- 3 **tablespoons lime juice**
- 10 **kaiser or onion rolls, split**

1. Place onions in a 4- or 5-qt. slow cooker. Mix brown sugar, paprika, salt and pepper; rub over roast. Place over the onions.

2. In a small bowl, mix broth, vinegar, soy sauce, Worcestershire sauce, chili sauce, molasses, garlic and mustard; pour over the roast. Cook, covered, on low for 8-10 hours or until the meat is tender.

3. Remove the roast; cool slightly. Skim fat from the cooking juices. In a small bowl, toss coleslaw mix with lime juice. Shred the pork with two forks. Return pork to slow cooker; heat through. Serve on rolls with the coleslaw.

BEEF
ENTREES

CHIPOTLE CARNE GUISADA

It's nice to have a meal that is both easy to prepare and sure to please. This is my go-to dinner when I have guests.
—**ADRIENNE SPENRATH** AUSTIN, TX

PREP: 30 MIN. • **COOK:** 6 HOURS
MAKES: 8 SERVINGS

- 2 **tablespoons canola oil**
- 2½ **pounds beef stew meat**
- 1 **can (8 ounces) tomato sauce**
- ¾ **cup water**
- 2 **chopped chipotle peppers in adobo sauce plus 2 tablespoons sauce**
- 12 **garlic cloves, minced**
- 1 **tablespoon chili powder**
- 1½ **teaspoons ground cumin**
- 1 **teaspoon beef bouillon granules**
- ½ **teaspoon pepper**
- ¼ **teaspoon salt**
  Hot cooked rice or warmed flour tortillas, optional

1. In a large skillet, heat oil over medium-high heat. Brown beef in batches. Transfer the meat to a 3-qt. slow cooker. Stir in tomato sauce, water, chipotle peppers, adobo sauce, garlic, chili powder, cumin, bouillon, pepper and salt.

2. Cook, covered, on low for 6-8 hours or until the meat is tender. If desired, serve with rice.

NOTES

SWEET & TANGY BEEF ROAST

PREP: 10 MIN. • **COOK:** 7 HOURS + STANDING
MAKES: 8 SERVINGS

- 1 tablespoon canola oil
- 1 boneless beef chuck roast (4 pounds)
- 2 medium onions, sliced into ½-inch rings
- 1 cup plus 2 tablespoons water, divided
- ¾ cup honey barbecue sauce
- ½ cup red pepper jelly
- 3 tablespoons hoisin sauce
- 2 tablespoons cornstarch

1. In a large skillet, heat oil over medium heat. Brown roast on all sides. Transfer to a 5-qt. slow cooker; add onions and 1 cup water.

2. In a small bowl, mix barbecue sauce, jelly and hoisin sauce; pour over the meat. Cook, covered, on low for 7-9 hours or until the meat is tender. Remove roast from slow cooker; tent with foil. Let stand 10 minutes before slicing.

3. Meanwhile, skim fat from cooking juices; transfer the juices to a small saucepan. Bring to a boil. Mix cornstarch and remaining water until smooth. Stir into the pan. Return to a boil; cook and stir for 1-2 minutes or until thickened. Serve with roast and onions.

This is a tasty change to the classic beef roast. I love to serve this for family dinners because I know it will be well-appreciated.

—**RACHEL VAN ORDEN** ANNVILLE, PA

HELPFUL HINT

It's not technically necessary to brown your meat before cooking it in a slow cooker, but the extra step will give the meat more depth of flavor, and is worth the time.

EASY ROPA VIEJA

Use your slow cooker for this meaty Cuban classic, which offers bold flavors without a lot of hands-on time.
—DENISE NYLAND PANAMA CITY, FL

PREP: 25 MIN. • **COOK:** 6 HOURS • **MAKES:** 8 SERVINGS

- 1 boneless beef chuck roast (2 pounds), cut in half
- 2 tablespoons olive oil
- 2 large onions, coarsely chopped
- 2 large green peppers, coarsely chopped
- 4 jalapeno peppers, seeded and minced
- 1 habanero pepper, seeded and minced
- 3 cans (14½ ounces each) diced tomatoes, undrained
- ½ cup water
- 6 garlic cloves, minced
- 2 tablespoons minced fresh cilantro
- 4 teaspoons beef bouillon granules
- 2 teaspoons pepper
- 1½ teaspoons ground cumin
- 1 teaspoon dried oregano
- ½ cup pimiento-stuffed olives, coarsely chopped
   Hot cooked rice, optional

1. In a large skillet, brown beef in oil on all sides. Transfer the meat to a 5-qt. slow cooker. Add onions and peppers. Combine tomatoes, water, garlic, cilantro, beef bouillon, pepper, cumin and oregano; pour over vegetables.

2. Cover and cook on low for 6-8 hours or until the meat is tender. Remove the beef; cool slightly. Skim fat from cooking juices; stir in olives. Shred the beef with two forks and return to the slow cooker; heat through. Serve with rice if desired.

FREEZE OPTION *Transfer individual portions of cooled stew to freezer containers and freeze. To use, partially thaw in refrigerator overnight. Heat through in a saucepan, stirring occasionally and adding a little water if necessary.*

NOTE *Wear disposable gloves when cutting hot peppers; the oils can burn skin. Avoid touching your face.*

SHORTCUT MEATBALL STEW

PREP: 20 MIN. • **COOK:** 9 HOURS
MAKES: 6 SERVINGS

- 3 medium potatoes, peeled and cut into ½-inch cubes
- 1 pound fresh baby carrots, quartered
- 1 large onion, chopped
- 3 celery ribs, sliced
- 1 package (12 ounces) frozen fully cooked home-style meatballs
- 1 can (10¾ ounces) condensed tomato soup, undiluted
- 1 can (10½ ounces) beef gravy
- 1 cup water
- 1 envelope onion soup mix
- 2 teaspoons beef bouillon granules

1. Place the potatoes, carrots, onion, celery and meatballs in a 5-qt. slow cooker. Combine the remaining ingredients; pour over the meatball mixture.
2. Cover and cook on low for 9-10 hours or until the vegetables are crisp-tender.

I came up with this meal as another way to use frozen meatballs. It's quick to put together in the morning and ready when my husband gets home in the evening.

—**IRIS SCHULTZ** MIAMISBURG, OH

BEEF & BEAN TORTA

This zesty dish is a favorite of mine because it has a wonderful Southwestern taste and is easy to prepare. I serve it on nights when we have only a few minutes to eat before running off to meetings or sports events.

—JOAN HALLFORD NORTH RICHLAND HILLS, TX

PREP: 30 MIN. • **COOK:** 4 HOURS • **MAKES:** 4 SERVINGS

- 1 **pound ground beef**
- 1 **small onion, chopped**
- 1 **can (15 ounces) pinto or black beans, rinsed and drained**
- 1 **can (10 ounces) diced tomatoes and green chilies, undrained**
- 1 **can (2¼ ounces) sliced ripe olives, drained**
- 1½ **teaspoons chili powder**
- ½ **teaspoon salt**
- ⅛ **teaspoon pepper**
- 3 **drops hot pepper sauce**
- 4 **flour tortillas (8 inches)**
- 1 **cup shredded cheddar cheese**
  Minced fresh cilantro, optional
  Salsa, sour cream, shredded lettuce and chopped tomatoes, optional

1. Cut four 20x3-in. strips of heavy-duty foil; crisscross so they resemble spokes of a wheel. Place foil strips on the bottom and up the sides of a 5-qt. slow cooker. Coat strips with cooking spray.

2. In a large skillet, cook beef and onion over medium heat until the meat is no longer pink; drain. Stir in beans, tomatoes, olives, chili powder, salt, pepper and hot pepper sauce. Spoon about 1⅔ cups into the prepared slow cooker; top with one tortilla and ¼ cup cheese. Repeat layers three times.

3. Cover and cook on low for 4-5 hours or until heated through. Using foil strips as handles, remove the tortilla stack to a platter. Sprinkle with cilantro. Serve with salsa, sour cream, lettuce and tomatoes if desired.

SLOW COOKER PIZZA CASSEROLE

PREP: 20 MIN. • **COOK:** 2 HOURS • **MAKES:** 14 SERVINGS

- 1 **package (16 ounces) rigatoni or large tube pasta**
- 1½ **pounds ground beef**
- 1 **small onion, chopped**
- 4 **cups shredded part-skim mozzarella cheese**
- 2 **cans (15 ounces each) pizza sauce**
- 1 **can (10¾ ounces) condensed cream of mushroom soup, undiluted**
- 1 **package (8 ounces) sliced pepperoni**

1. Cook pasta according to package directions. Meanwhile, in a skillet, cook beef and onion over medium heat until the meat is no longer pink; drain.

2. Drain the pasta; place in a 5-qt. slow cooker. Stir in the beef mixture, cheese, pizza sauce, soup and pepperoni. Cover and cook on low for 2-3 hours or until heated through.

A comforting casserole with mass appeal is just what you need when cooking for a crowd. For added convenience, it stays warm in a slow cooker.

—**VIRGINIA KRITES** CRIDERSVILLE, OH

HELPFUL HINT

Slow cookers come with either metal or crockery inserts. Our recipes were tested using the crockery type. If you're using the metal type, you may need to stir occasionally to keep food from sticking; add 15 minutes to the cooking time each time you open the lid.

BEEF & RICE STUFFED CABBAGE ROLLS

My family is quick to come to the table when I serve my cabbage rolls. They are simple to make and really satisfy without being too fattening.

—LYNN BOWEN GERALDINE, AL

PREP: 20 MIN. • **COOK:** 6 HOURS • **MAKES:** 6 SERVINGS

- 12 **cabbage leaves**
- 1 **cup cooked brown rice**
- ¼ **cup finely chopped onion**
- 1 **large egg, lightly beaten**
- ¼ **cup fat-free milk**
- ½ **teaspoon salt**
- ¼ **teaspoon pepper**
- 1 **pound lean ground beef (90% lean)**

SAUCE
- 1 **can (8 ounces) tomato sauce**
- 1 **tablespoon brown sugar**
- 1 **tablespoon lemon juice**
- 1 **teaspoon Worcestershire sauce**

1. In batches, cook cabbage in boiling water for 3-5 minutes or until crisp-tender. Drain; cool slightly. Trim the thick vein from the bottom of each cabbage leaf, making a V-shaped cut.

2. In a large bowl, combine rice, onion, egg, milk, salt and pepper. Add beef; mix lightly but thoroughly. Place about ¼ cup of the beef mixture on each cabbage leaf. Pull together the cut edges of the leaf to overlap; fold over filling. Fold in the sides and roll up.

3. Place six rolls in a 4- or 5-qt. slow cooker, seam side down. In a bowl, mix sauce ingredients; pour half of the sauce over the cabbage rolls. Top with the remaining rolls and sauce. Cook, covered, on low for 6-8 hours or until a thermometer inserted in the beef reads 160° and the cabbage is tender.

SLOW-COOKED SWISS STEAK

PREP: 10 MIN. • **COOK:** 6 HOURS • **MAKES:** 6 SERVINGS

- 2 **tablespoons all-purpose flour**
- ½ **teaspoon salt**
- ¼ **teaspoon pepper**
- 1½ **pounds beef round steak, cut into six pieces**
- 1 **medium onion, cut into ¼-inch slices**
- 1 **celery rib, cut into ½-inch slices**
- 2 **cans (8 ounces each) tomato sauce**

1. In a large resealable plastic bag, combine flour, salt and pepper. Add steak; seal bag and shake to coat.

2. Place onion in a greased 3-qt. slow cooker. Top with the steak, celery and tomato sauce. Cover and cook on low for 6-8 hours or until the meat is tender.

This is one of my favorites to make because I can flour and season the steaks and refrigerate them overnight. The next morning, I just put all the ingredients in the slow cooker, and I have a delicious dinner waiting when I arrive home from work.

—SARAH BURKS WATHENA, KS

HELPFUL HINT

Overfilling a slow cooker will affect cooking time. Check manufacturer instructions for their recommendation; the rule of thumb is to fill no more than two-thirds full.

TACO MEAT LOAF

Our children think there are three basic food groups—pizza, tacos and burgers! They like to doctor up slices of this meat loaf with their favorite taco toppings.
—DIANE ESSINGER FINDLAY, OH

PREP: 10 MIN. • **COOK:** 8 HOURS • **MAKES:** 8 SERVINGS

- 1 **large egg, beaten**
- ½ **cup sour cream**
- ⅓ **cup salsa**
- 2 **to 4 tablespoons taco seasoning**
- 1 **cup crushed tortilla chips**
- ½ **cup shredded cheddar cheese**
- 2 **pounds lean ground beef (90% lean)**
  Optional toppings: sour cream, salsa, shredded cheddar cheese, shredded lettuce, sliced ripe olives

1. In a large bowl, combine the first six ingredients. Crumble beef over mixture and mix well. Pat into a 3-qt. slow cooker.
2. Cover and cook on low for 8 hours or until no pink remains and a thermometer reads 160°. Top with sour cream, salsa, cheese, lettuce and olives if desired.

NOTES

SUPER SHORT RIBS

This came from an old oven recipe my mom had for short ribs.
I added a few ingredients to the original to suit my taste.
—COLEEN CARTER MALONE, NY

PREP: 20 MIN. • **COOK:** 8 HOURS • **MAKES:** 6 SERVINGS

- 3 **medium onions, cut into wedges**
- 3 **to 3½ pounds bone-in beef short ribs**
- 1 **bay leaf**
- 1 **bottle (12 ounces) beer or nonalcoholic beer**
- 2 **tablespoons brown sugar**
- 2 **tablespoons Dijon mustard**
- 2 **tablespoons tomato paste**
- 2 **teaspoons dried thyme**
- 2 **teaspoons beef bouillon granules**
- 1 **teaspoon salt**
- ¼ **teaspoon pepper**
- 3 **tablespoons all-purpose flour**
- ½ **cup cold water**
  Hot cooked noodles

1. Place onions in a 5-qt. slow cooker; add ribs and bay leaf.
Combine beer, brown sugar, mustard, tomato paste, thyme,
bouillon, salt and pepper. Pour over the meat.

2. Cover and cook on low for 8-10 hours or until the meat
is tender.

3. Remove the meat and vegetables to a serving platter; keep
warm. Discard the bay leaf. Skim fat from cooking juices;
transfer the juices to a small saucepan. Bring to a boil.

4. Combine flour and water until smooth. Gradually stir into
the pan. Bring to a boil; cook and stir for 2 minutes or until
thickened. Serve with the meat and noodles.

FABULOUS FAJITAS

I've enjoyed cooking since I was a girl growing up in the Southwest. When friends call to ask me for new recipes to try, I suggest these flavorful fajitas. It's wonderful being able to put the beef in the slow cooker before church and come home to a hot, delicious main dish.
—JANIE REITZ ROCHESTER, MN

PREP: 20 MIN. • **COOK:** 3 HOURS • **MAKES:** 8 SERVINGS

- 1½ **pounds beef top sirloin steak, cut into thin strips**
- 2 **tablespoons canola oil**
- 2 **tablespoons lemon juice**
- 1 **garlic clove, minced**
- 1½ **teaspoons ground cumin**
- 1 **teaspoon seasoned salt**
- ½ **teaspoon chili powder**
- ¼ **to ½ teaspoon crushed red pepper flakes**
- 1 **large green pepper, julienned**
- 1 **large onion, julienned**
- 8 **flour tortillas (8 inches)**
  Shredded cheddar cheese, salsa, sour cream, lettuce and tomatoes, optional

1. In a large skillet, brown steak in oil over medium heat. Place the steak and drippings in a 3-qt. slow cooker. Stir in lemon juice, garlic, cumin, salt, chili powder and red pepper flakes.

2. Cover and cook on high for 2-3 hours or until the meat is almost tender. Add green pepper and onion; cover and cook for 1 hour or until meat and vegetables are tender.

3. Warm tortillas according to package directions; spoon beef and vegetables down center of tortillas. Top with cheese, salsa, sour cream, lettuce and tomatoes if desired.

COFFEE-BRAISED ROAST BEEF

This recipe has been a family tradition since 1974. The meat is quick to make and flavorful, so it's a nice welcome home after a long day of work. The coffee adds an intriguing flavor to the roast and can be thickened for a delicious gravy.

—NANCY SCHULER BELLE FOURCHE, SD

PREP: 10 MIN. + MARINATING • **COOK:** 6½ HOURS
MAKES: 10 SERVINGS

- 1 **cup cider vinegar**
- 4 **garlic cloves, crushed, divided**
- 1 **boneless beef chuck roast (4 to 5 pounds), trimmed**
- 2 **teaspoons salt**
- 1 **teaspoon pepper**
- 1 **cup strong brewed coffee**
- 1 **cup beef broth**
- 1 **medium onion, sliced**
- 3 **tablespoons cornstarch**
- ¼ **cup cold water**
  Mashed potatoes

1. In a large resealable plastic bag, combine vinegar and 2 garlic cloves. Add roast; seal bag and turn to coat. Refrigerate overnight, turning occasionally.

2. Drain and discard marinade. Pat the roast dry; sprinkle with salt and pepper. Place in a 5- or 6-qt. slow cooker; add coffee, broth, onion and remaining garlic. Cook, covered, on low for 6-7 hours or until the meat is tender.

3. Remove the roast and keep warm. Strain cooking juices, discarding the onion and garlic; skim fat. In a small bowl, mix cornstarch and cold water until smooth; gradually stir into slow cooker. Cook, covered, on high for 30 minutes or until the gravy is thickened. Slice the roast; serve with mashed potatoes and gravy.

TOMATO-BASIL STEAK

PREP: 15 MIN. • **COOK:** 6 HOURS
MAKES: 4 SERVINGS

1¼ **pounds boneless beef shoulder top blade or flat iron steaks**
½ **pound whole fresh mushrooms, quartered**
1 **medium sweet yellow pepper, julienned**
1 **can (14½ ounces) stewed tomatoes, undrained**
1 **can (8 ounces) tomato sauce**
1 **envelope onion soup mix**
2 **tablespoons minced fresh basil**
Hot cooked rice

1. Place steaks in a 4-qt. slow cooker. Add mushrooms and pepper. In a small bowl, mix tomatoes, tomato sauce, soup mix and basil; pour over top.
2. Cook, covered, on low for 6-8 hours or until the beef and vegetables are tender. Serve with rice.

I use basil and bell peppers from my herb and vegetable garden to make this dish. It's so easy to prepare and so rich and delicious.

—**SHERRY LITTLE** SHERWOOD, AR

MEXICAN BUBBLE PIZZA

This tasty pizza offers a new way to experience Mexican cuisine. Serve it at your next party and watch it disappear before your eyes.

—JACKIE HANNAHS CEDAR SPRINGS, MI

PREP: 15 MIN. • **COOK:** 3 HOURS • **MAKES:** 6 SERVINGS

- 1½ **pounds ground beef**
- 1 **can (10¾ ounces) condensed tomato soup, undiluted**
- ¾ **cup water**
- 1 **envelope taco seasoning**
- 1 **tube (16.3 ounces) large refrigerated buttermilk biscuits**
- 2 **cups shredded cheddar cheese**
  Optional toppings: shredded lettuce, chopped tomatoes, salsa, sliced ripe olives, sour cream and thinly sliced green onions

1. Fold an 18-in. square piece of heavy-duty foil in half to make an 18x9-in. strip. Place strip on bottom and up sides of a 6-qt. slow cooker. Coat the strip with cooking spray.

2. In a large skillet, cook ground beef over medium heat for 6-8 minutes or until no longer pink, breaking into crumbles; drain. Stir in soup, water and taco seasoning. Bring to a boil. Reduce heat; simmer, uncovered, for 3-5 minutes or until slightly thickened.

3. Cut each biscuit into four pieces; gently stir into the beef mixture. Transfer to the slow cooker. Cook, covered, on low for 3-4 hours or until dough is cooked through. Sprinkle with cheese. Cook, covered, 5 minutes longer or until the cheese is melted. Serve with toppings of your choice.

SLOW COOKER GROUND BEEF STROGANOFF

My mother gave me this recipe 40 years ago. It's a wonderful, tasty dish to share around the dinner table.
—**SUE MIMS** MACCLENNY, FL

PREP: 25 MIN. • **COOK:** 4¼ HOURS • **MAKES:** 8 SERVINGS

- 2 pounds ground beef
- 1½ teaspoons salt
- 1 teaspoon pepper
- 1 tablespoon butter
- ½ pound sliced fresh mushrooms
- 2 medium onions, chopped
- 2 garlic cloves, minced
- 1 can (10½ ounces) condensed beef consomme, undiluted
- ⅓ cup all-purpose flour
- 2 tablespoons tomato paste
- 1½ cups (12 ounces) sour cream
    Hot cooked noodles

1. In a large skillet, cook beef, salt and pepper over medium heat for 6-8 minutes or until the meat is no longer pink, breaking into crumbles; drain. Transfer meat to a 3- or 4-qt. slow cooker.

2. In the same skillet, heat butter over medium-high heat. Add mushrooms and onions; cook and stir for 6-8 minutes or until the onions are tender and the mushrooms have released their liquid and begin to brown. Add garlic; cook 1 minute longer. Transfer to the slow cooker.

3. In a small bowl, whisk together consomme, flour and tomato paste. Pour over the meat mixture; stir to combine. Cook, covered, on low for 4-6 hours or until thickened. Stir in sour cream. Cook, covered, 15-30 minutes longer or until heated through. Serve with noodles.

SPINACH & FETA STUFFED FLANK STEAK

If you need a main dish recipe with an upscale feel, this slow-cooked dish is a great choice. Elegant enough for company, the rolled flank steak looks pretty on a plate.

—STEVEN SCHEND GRAND RAPIDS, MI

PREP: 30 MIN. • **COOK:** 6 HOURS
MAKES: 6 SERVINGS

- 1 **beef flank steak (1½ pounds)**
- 2 **cups crumbled feta cheese**
- 3 **cups fresh baby spinach**
- ½ **cup oil-packed sun-dried tomatoes, drained and chopped**
- ½ **cup finely chopped onion**
- 5 **tablespoons all-purpose flour, divided**
- ½ **teaspoon salt**
- ½ **teaspoon pepper**
- 2 **tablespoons canola oil**
- 1 **cup beef broth**
- 1 **tablespoon Worcestershire sauce**
- 2 **teaspoons tomato paste**
- ⅓ **cup dry red wine or additional beef broth**
  Hot cooked egg noodles, optional

1. Starting at one long side, cut steak horizontally in half to within ½ in. of opposite side. Open steak flat; cover with plastic wrap. Pound with a meat mallet to ½-in. thickness. Remove the plastic.

2. Sprinkle 1 cup cheese over the steak to within 1 in. of edges. Layer with spinach, tomatoes, onion and remaining cheese. Roll up jelly-roll style, starting with a long side; tie at 1½-in. intervals with kitchen string. Sprinkle with 2 tablespoons flour, salt and pepper.

3. In a large skillet, heat oil over medium heat. Brown the beef on all sides; drain. Transfer to a 6-qt. oval slow cooker. In a small bowl, mix broth, Worcestershire sauce and tomato paste; pour over top. Cook, covered, on low for 6-8 hours or until the meat is tender.

4. Remove the beef to a platter; keep warm. Transfer cooking juices to a small saucepan; skim fat. Bring the juices to a boil. Mix the remaining flour and red wine until smooth; gradually stir into pan. Return to a boil; cook and stir for 1-2 minutes or until thickened. Serve the beef with gravy and, if desired, noodles.

CHILE COLORADO BURRITOS

PREP: 20 MIN. • **COOK:** 6¼ HOURS • **MAKES:** 8 SERVINGS

- **2 pounds boneless beef chuck roast, cut into 1½-inch pieces**
- **2 cans (10 ounces each) enchilada sauce**
- **1 teaspoon beef bouillon granules**
- **1 can (16 ounces) refried beans, optional**
- **8 flour tortillas (8 inches)**
- **1 cup shredded Colby-Monterey Jack cheese**
  Chopped green onions, optional

1. In a 4-qt. slow cooker, combine beef, enchilada sauce and bouillon granules. Cook, covered, on low for 6-8 hours or until the meat is tender.

2. Preheat oven to 425°. Using a slotted spoon, remove the meat from sauce. Skim fat from the sauce. If desired, spoon about ¼ cup beans across center of each tortilla; top with ⅓ cup meat. Fold bottom and sides of the tortilla over the filling and roll up.

3. Place the filled tortillas in a greased 11x7-in. baking dish. Pour 1 cup sauce over top; sprinkle with cheese. Bake, uncovered, 10-15 minutes or until cheese is melted. If desired, sprinkle with green onions.

When I was growing up in Southern California, this was one of my favorite Mexican dishes. It's hard to find now that I live in the Midwest—except in my kitchen!

—**KELLY MCCULLEY** DES MOINES, IA

ASIAN-STYLE ROUND STEAK

My friend gave me this recipe more than two decades ago and all I added was a little extra meat, celery and mushrooms. I have long relied on this dish to satisfy my family at mealtimes.
—MARILYN WOLFE DES MOINES, IA

PREP: 20 MIN. • **COOK:** 7 HOURS • **MAKES:** 8 SERVINGS

- 2 **pounds beef top round steak, cut into 3-inch strips**
- 2 **tablespoons canola oil**
- 3 **celery ribs, chopped**
- 1 **cup chopped onion**
- ¼ **cup reduced-sodium soy sauce**
- 1 **teaspoon sugar**
- ½ **teaspoon salt**
- ½ **teaspoon minced garlic**
- ¼ **teaspoon ground ginger**
- ¼ **teaspoon pepper**
- 2 **medium green peppers, julienned**
- 1 **can (15 ounces) tomato sauce**
- 1 **can (14 ounces) bean sprouts, rinsed and drained**
- 1 **can (8 ounces) sliced water chestnuts, drained**
- 1 **jar (4½ ounces) sliced mushrooms, drained**
- 1 **tablespoon cornstarch**
- ½ **cup cold water**
  Hot cooked rice

1. In a large skillet, brown meat in oil on all sides. Transfer the meat and drippings to a 5-qt. slow cooker. Combine celery, onion, soy sauce, sugar, salt, garlic, ginger and pepper; pour over the meat. Cover and cook on low for 5½-6 hours or until the meat is tender.

2. Add green peppers, tomato sauce, bean sprouts, water chestnuts and mushrooms; cover and cook on low for 1 hour longer.

3. Combine cornstarch and water until smooth; stir into the beef mixture. Cover and cook on high for 30 minutes or until the sauce is thickened. Serve with rice.

STEAK SAN MARINO

As a busy pastor's wife and mother of three, I rely on this delicious, inexpensive dish to help my day run smoother. The steak is so tender and flavorful, my kids gobble it up and my husband asks for seconds.

—LAEL GRIESS HULL, IA

PREP: 15 MIN. • **COOK:** 7 HOURS • **MAKES:** 6 SERVINGS

- ¼ **cup all-purpose flour**
- ½ **teaspoon salt**
- ½ **teaspoon pepper**
- 1 **beef top round steak (1½ pounds), cut into six pieces**
- 2 **large carrots, sliced**
- 1 **celery rib, sliced**
- 1 **can (8 ounces) tomato sauce**
- 2 **garlic cloves, minced**
- 1 **bay leaf**
- 1 **teaspoon Italian seasoning**
- ½ **teaspoon Worcestershire sauce**
- 3 **cups hot cooked brown rice**

1. In a large resealable plastic bag, combine the flour, salt and pepper. Add beef, a few pieces at a time, and shake to coat. Transfer beef to a 4-qt. slow cooker.

2. In a small bowl, combine carrots, celery, tomato sauce, garlic, bay leaf, Italian seasoning and Worcestershire sauce. Pour over the beef. Cover and cook on low for 7-9 hours or until the beef is tender. Discard the bay leaf. Serve with rice.

FREEZE OPTION *Place cooked steak and vegetables in freezer containers; top with sauce. Cool, then freeze. To use, partially thaw in refrigerator overnight. Heat through in a covered saucepan, gently stirring and adding a little water if necessary.*

STEPHANIE'S SLOW COOKER STEW

Start this warming one-pot meal before you head out for the day. By the time you get home, the well-seasoned meat will be tender and mouthwatering.

—STEPHANIE RABBITT-SCHAPP

CINCINNATI, OH

PREP: 20 MIN. • **COOK:** 7½ HOURS
MAKES: 5 SERVINGS

- 1 **pound beef stew meat**
- 2 **medium potatoes, peeled and cubed**
- 1 **can (14½ ounces) beef broth**
- 1 **can (11½ ounces) V8 juice**
- 2 **celery ribs, chopped**
- 2 **medium carrots, chopped**
- 1 **medium sweet onion, chopped**
- 3 **bay leaves**
- ½ **teaspoon salt**
- ½ **teaspoon dried thyme**
- ½ **teaspoon chili powder**
- ¼ **teaspoon pepper**
- 2 **tablespoons cornstarch**
- 1 **tablespoon cold water**
- ½ **cup frozen corn**
- ½ **cup frozen peas**

1. In a 3-qt. slow cooker, combine the first 12 ingredients. Cover and cook on low for 7-8 hours or until the meat is tender. Discard the bay leaves.

2. In a small bowl, combine cornstarch and water until smooth; stir into the stew. Add corn and peas. Cover and cook on high for 30 minutes or until thickened.

SLOW COOKER ENCHILADAS

PREP: 30 MIN. • **COOK:** 5 HOURS • **MAKES:** 4 SERVINGS

- 1 **pound ground beef**
- 1 **cup chopped onion**
- ½ **cup chopped green pepper**
- 1 **can (16 ounces) pinto or kidney beans, rinsed and drained**
- 1 **can (15 ounces) black beans, rinsed and drained**
- 1 **can (10 ounces) diced tomatoes and green chilies, undrained**
- ⅓ **cup water**
- 1 **teaspoon chili powder**
- ½ **teaspoon ground cumin**
- ½ **teaspoon salt**
- ¼ **teaspoon pepper**
- 1 **cup shredded sharp cheddar cheese**
- 1 **cup shredded Monterey Jack cheese**
- 6 **flour tortillas (6 inches)**

1. In a large skillet, cook beef, onion and green pepper until the meat is no longer pink; drain. Add the next eight ingredients; bring to a boil. Reduce heat; cover and simmer for 10 minutes. Combine the cheeses.

2. In a 5-qt. slow cooker, layer about ¾ cup of the beef mixture, one tortilla and about ⅓ cup cheese. Repeat layers. Cover and cook on low for 5-7 hours or until heated through.

When you crave Southwestern food but don't want to spend time preparing it in the evening, this recipe will come in handy. It's a sensational supper for busy weeknights.

—MARY LUEBBERT BENTON, KS

STAMP-OF-APPROVAL SPAGHETTI SAUCE

My father is pretty opinionated, especially about food. This recipe received his nearly unattainable stamp of approval, and I have yet to hear any disagreement from anyone else who has tried it!

—MELISSA TAYLOR HIGLEY, AZ

PREP: 30 MIN. • **COOK:** 8 HOURS
MAKES: 12 SERVINGS (3 QUARTS)

- 2 **pounds ground beef**
- ¾ **pound bulk Italian sausage**
- 4 **medium onions, finely chopped**
- 8 **garlic cloves, minced**
- 4 **cans (14½ ounces each) diced tomatoes, undrained**
- 4 **cans (6 ounces each) tomato paste**
- ½ **cup water**
- ¼ **cup sugar**
- ¼ **cup Worcestershire sauce**
- 1 **tablespoon canola oil**
- ¼ **cup minced fresh parsley**
- 2 **tablespoons minced fresh basil or 2 teaspoons dried basil**
- 1 **tablespoon minced fresh oregano or 1 teaspoon dried oregano**
- 4 **bay leaves**
- 1 **teaspoon rubbed sage**
- ½ **teaspoon salt**
- ½ **teaspoon dried marjoram**
- ½ **teaspoon pepper**
  Hot cooked spaghetti

1. In a Dutch oven, cook beef, sausage, onions and garlic over medium heat until the meat is no longer pink; drain.

2. Transfer to a 5-qt. slow cooker. Stir in tomatoes, tomato paste, water, sugar, Worcestershire sauce, oil and seasonings.

3. Cover and cook on low for 8-10 hours. Discard the bay leaves. Serve with spaghetti.

FREEZE OPTION *Cool before placing in a freezer container. Cover and freeze for up to 3 months. To use, thaw in the refrigerator overnight. Place in a large saucepan; heat through, stirring occasionally. Serve with spaghetti.*

CHICKEN & TURKEY
FAVORITES

BROCCOLI-CAULIFLOWER CHICKEN CASSEROLE

This is one of our favorite comfort dishes. I make my simple variation in the slow cooker with no rice. You can easily swap in whatever cheese you prefer, I sometimes use dairy-free cheese to create a more paleo-friendly dinner. The dish is also delicious sprinkled with a simple bread crumb topping.

—COURTNEY STULTZ WEIR, KS

PREP: 20 MIN. • **COOK:** 4 HOURS
MAKES: 8 SERVINGS

- 2 **pounds boneless skinless chicken breasts, cut into 1-inch pieces**
- 1 **small head cauliflower, chopped (about 4 cups)**
- 1 **bunch broccoli, chopped (about 4 cups)**
- ½ **pound medium fresh mushrooms, chopped**
- 1 **large onion, chopped**
- 2 **medium carrots, finely chopped**
- 1 **cup reduced-sodium chicken broth**
- 4 **ounces cream cheese, softened**
- 2 **tablespoons olive oil**
- 2 **teaspoons dried sage leaves**
- 1 **teaspoon salt**
- ½ **teaspoon pepper**
- 1 **cup shredded cheddar cheese**
  Hot cooked brown rice

In a 6-qt. slow cooker, combine the first six ingredients. In a small bowl, whisk broth, cream cheese, oil, sage, salt and pepper; pour over the chicken mixture. Sprinkle with cheese. Cook, covered, on low for 4-5 hours or until the chicken and vegetables are tender. Serve with rice.

HERBED TURKEY BREASTS

PREP: 25 MIN. + MARINATING • **COOK:** 3½ HOURS
MAKES: 12 SERVINGS

- 1 **can (14½ ounces) chicken broth**
- ½ **cup lemon juice**
- ¼ **cup packed brown sugar**
- ¼ **cup fresh sage**
- ¼ **cup fresh thyme leaves**
- ¼ **cup lime juice**
- ¼ **cup cider vinegar**
- ¼ **cup olive oil**
- 1 **envelope onion soup mix**
- 2 **tablespoons Dijon mustard**
- 1 **tablespoon minced fresh marjoram**
- 1½ **teaspoons paprika**
- 1 **teaspoon garlic powder**
- 1 **teaspoon pepper**
- ½ **teaspoon salt**
- 2 **boneless skinless turkey breast halves (2 pounds each)**

1. In a blender, process the first 15 ingredients until blended. Pour marinade into a large resealable plastic bag; add the turkey. Seal bag and turn to coat; refrigerate for 8 hours or overnight.

2. Transfer turkey and marinade to a 5-qt. slow cooker. Cover and cook on high for 3½-4½ hours or until a thermometer reads 165°.

Tender, moist turkey breast is enhanced with an array of flavorful herbs in this comforting slow cooker recipe.

—**LAURIE MACE** LOS OSOS, CA

CHEESY TURKEY MEAT LOAF

Nothing says comfort food better than meat loaf! Get this one started in the morning, and you'll have a delicious hot meal ready by lunchtime.

—DEANNA LAUGHINGHOUSE RALEIGH, NC

PREP: 15 MIN. • **COOK:** 3 HOURS + STANDING
MAKES: 6 SERVINGS

- 1 **large egg, lightly beaten**
- 1 **cup crushed saltines**
- 1 **cup ketchup**
- 2 **garlic cloves, minced**
- 1 **teaspoon salt**
- 1 **teaspoon pepper**
- 2 **pounds ground turkey**
- 2½ **cups shredded cheddar cheese, divided**
- ½ **cup shredded Parmesan cheese**

1. Fold an 18-in. square piece of heavy-duty foil in half to make an 18x9-in. strip. Place foil strip on bottom and up sides of a 5- or 6-qt. slow cooker. Coat strip with cooking spray.

2. In a large bowl, combine the first six ingredients. Add turkey, 2 cups cheddar cheese and Parmesan cheese; mix lightly but thoroughly (mixture will be moist). Shape into an 8x5-in. loaf; place in the center of the strip.

3. Cook, covered, on low 3-4 hours or until a thermometer reads 165°. Sprinkle with the remaining cheese during the last 20 minutes of cooking. Using ends of foil strip as handles, remove the meat loaf to a platter. Let stand 15 minutes.

FREEZE OPTION *Prepare and cook meat loaf as directed, omitting the cheddar cheese over top. Securely wrap cooled meat loaf in plastic wrap and foil, then freeze; freeze cheese in a freezer container. To use, partially thaw in refrigerator overnight. Unwrap meat loaf; reheat on a greased 15x10x1-in. baking pan in a preheated 350° oven until heated through and a thermometer inserted in center reads 165°. Sprinkle with cheese.*

ZESTY SOUTHWEST CHICKEN

PREP: 10 MIN. • **COOK:** 6 HOURS
MAKES: 6 SERVINGS

2 cans (15¼ ounces each) whole kernel corn, drained
1 can (15 ounces) black beans, rinsed and drained
1 jar (16 ounces) chunky salsa
6 boneless skinless chicken breast halves (4 ounces each)
1 cup (4 ounces) shredded cheddar cheese

1. In a 5-qt. slow cooker, combine corn, black beans and ½ cup salsa. Top with chicken and remaining salsa.
2. Cover and cook on low for 6-8 hours or until the chicken is tender. Sprinkle with cheese. Cover and cook 5 minutes longer or until the cheese is melted.

Prepared salsa and convenient canned corn and beans add fun color, texture and flavor to this chicken dish. I usually serve it with salad and white rice. Our children love it!

—**KAREN WATERS** LAUREL, MD

CHICKEN TIKKA MASALA

This Indian-style dish has flavors that keep me coming back for more—it's a simple dish spiced with garam masala, cumin and gingerroot that's simply amazing.
—JACLYN BELL LOGAN, UT

PREP: 25 MIN. • **COOK:** 4¼ HOURS • **MAKES:** 8 SERVINGS

- 1 can (29 ounces) tomato puree
- 1½ cups (12 ounces) plain yogurt
- ½ large onion, finely chopped
- 2 tablespoons olive oil
- 4½ teaspoons minced fresh gingerroot
- 4 garlic cloves, minced
- 1 tablespoon garam masala
- 2½ teaspoons salt
- 1½ teaspoons ground cumin
- 1 teaspoon paprika
- ¾ teaspoon pepper
- ½ teaspoon cayenne pepper
- ¼ teaspoon ground cinnamon
- 2½ pounds boneless skinless chicken breasts, cut into 1½-inch cubes
- 1 jalapeno pepper, halved and seeded
- 1 bay leaf
- 1 tablespoon cornstarch
- 1 cup heavy whipping cream
  Hot cooked basmati rice
  Chopped fresh cilantro, optional

1. In a 5-qt. slow cooker, combine the first 13 ingredients. Add chicken, jalapeno and bay leaf. Cook, covered, on low for 4 hours or until the chicken is tender. Remove the jalapeno and bay leaf.

2. In a small bowl, mix cornstarch and cream until smooth; gradually stir into the sauce. Cook, covered, on high for 15-20 minutes or until the sauce is thickened. Serve with rice. If desired, sprinkle with cilantro.

NOTE *Wear disposable gloves when cutting hot peppers; the oils can burn skin. Avoid touching your face.*

TURKEY TACO MACARONI

PREP: 15 MIN. • **COOK:** 3 HOURS + STANDING
MAKES: 10 SERVINGS

- 2 **tablespoons canola oil, divided**
- 4 **cups uncooked elbow macaroni**
- 2 **pounds ground turkey**
- 1 **medium onion, chopped**
- 4 **cans (8 ounces each) tomato sauce**
- 1 **cup water**
- 1 **cup salsa**
- 1 **envelope taco seasoning**
- 2 **cups (8 ounces) shredded cheddar cheese**

1. In a large skillet, heat 1 tablespoon oil over medium heat. Add pasta; cook and stir for 2-3 minutes or until the pasta is toasted. Transfer to a 5-qt. slow cooker. In the same skillet, heat remaining oil over medium-high heat. Add turkey and onion; cook 6-8 minutes or until the meat is no longer pink, breaking into crumbles.

2. Transfer to the slow cooker. Stir in tomato sauce, water, salsa and taco seasoning. Cook, covered, for 3-4 hours or until the pasta is tender.

3. Remove slow cooker insert; top with cheese. Let stand, covered, for 15 minutes before serving.

This is a nice twist on a classic dish. Green peppers are a great taste if you want some vegetables—and feel free to add more cheese.

—**BARB KONDOLF** HAMLIN, NY

SLOW COOKER CHEESY WHITE LASAGNA

Here's my best version of my favorite food—lasagna! The recipe is a winner, so it's worth the extra prep. You'll have plenty of time to plan side dishes while the main dish is cooking.
—**SUZANNE SMITH** BLUFFTON, IN

PREP: 30 MIN.
COOK: 3 HOURS + STANDING
MAKES: 8 SERVINGS

- 1 pound ground chicken or beef
- 2 teaspoons canola oil
- 1¾ cups sliced fresh mushrooms
- 1 medium onion, chopped
- 2 medium carrots, chopped
- 2 garlic cloves, minced
- 2 teaspoons Italian seasoning
- ¾ teaspoon salt
- ½ teaspoon pepper
- ½ cup white wine or chicken broth
- 1 cup half-and-half cream
- ½ cup cream cheese, softened
- 1 cup shredded white cheddar cheese
- 1 cup shredded Gouda cheese
- 1 large egg, beaten
- 1½ cups (12 ounces) 2% cottage cheese
- ¼ cup minced fresh basil or 4 teaspoons dried basil
- 9 no-cook lasagna noodles
- 4 cups shredded part-skim mozzarella cheese
  Additional minced fresh basil, optional

1. Fold two 18-in. square pieces of heavy-duty foil into thirds. Crisscross the strips and place on bottom and up sides of a 6-qt. slow cooker. Coat foil strips with cooking spray.

2. In a 6-qt. stockpot, cook chicken over medium heat until no longer pink, 6-8 minutes, breaking into crumbles; drain. Set chicken aside.

3. In the same pot, heat oil over medium-high heat. Add mushrooms, onion and carrots; cook and stir just until tender, 6-8 minutes. Add garlic, Italian seasoning, salt and pepper; cook 1 minute longer. Stir in wine. Bring to a boil; cook until liquid is reduced by half, 4-5 minutes. Stir in cream, cream cheese, cheddar and Gouda cheeses. Return chicken to the pot. In a large bowl, combine egg, cottage cheese and basil.

4. Spread 1 cup of the meat mixture into the slow cooker. Layer with 3 noodles (breaking noodles as necessary to fit), 1 cup meat mixture, ½ cup cottage cheese mixture and 1 cup mozzarella cheese. Repeat layers twice. Top with remaining meat mixture and cheese. Cook, covered, on low until the noodles are tender, 3-4 hours. Remove the slow cooker insert and let stand 30 minutes before serving. If desired, sprinkle with additional basil.

SOY-GINGER CHICKEN

Bone-in chicken becomes moist and tender when cooked with carrots and green onions in a rich ginger-soy sauce that's brightened with brown sugar, balsamic vinegar and coriander.
—**KAEL HARVEY** BROOKLYN, NY

PREP: 25 MIN. • **COOK:** 5 HOURS • **MAKES:** 4 SERVINGS

- **4 bone-in chicken thighs (about 1½ pounds), skin removed**
- **4 chicken drumsticks (about 1 pound), skin removed**
- **2 medium carrots, sliced**
- **4 green onions, thinly sliced**
- **⅓ cup soy sauce**
- **2 tablespoons brown sugar**
- **1 piece fresh gingerroot (about 2 inches), peeled and thinly sliced**
- **5 garlic cloves, minced**
- **1 tablespoon balsamic vinegar**
- **1 teaspoon ground coriander**
- **½ teaspoon pepper**
- **1 tablespoon cornstarch**
- **1 tablespoon cold water**
- **Hot cooked rice and minced fresh cilantro**

1. Place chicken, carrots and green onions in a 3-qt. slow cooker. Combine soy sauce, brown sugar, ginger, garlic, vinegar, coriander and pepper in a small bowl. Pour over top of the chicken. Cover and cook on low for 5-6 hours or until the chicken is tender.

2. Remove the chicken to a serving platter; keep warm. Pour juices into a small saucepan. Bring to a boil. Combine cornstarch and water until smooth; gradually stir into pan. Bring to a boil; cook and stir for 1-2 minutes or until thickened. Serve with chicken and rice; sprinkle servings with cilantro.

HELPFUL HINT

Unless the recipe calls for it, don't use aluminum foil in your slow cooker with tomatoes or other acidic foods. Acids will cause the aluminum to degrade during heating, which is not healthy.

UPSIDE-DOWN FRITO PIE

Using ground turkey is a smart way to lighten up this family pleaser!
—MARY BERG LAKE ELMO, MN

PREP: 15 MIN. • **COOK:** 2 HOURS • **MAKES:** 6 SERVINGS

- **2 pounds ground turkey or beef**
- **1 medium onion, chopped**
- **2 envelopes chili seasoning mix**
- **1 can (10 ounces) diced tomatoes and green chilies, undrained**
- **1 can (8 ounces) tomato sauce**
- **1 can (15 ounces) pinto beans, rinsed and drained**
- **1 cup shredded cheddar cheese**
- **3 cups corn chips**
  Sour cream, minced fresh cilantro and additional chopped onion, optional

1. In a large skillet, cook turkey and onion over medium heat for 8-10 minutes or until no longer pink, breaking into crumbles; stir in chili seasoning. Transfer to a 3- or 4-qt. slow cooker. Pour tomatoes and tomato sauce over the turkey.

2. Cook, covered, on low for 2-3 hours or until heated through. Stir the turkey mixture to combine. Top with beans. Sprinkle with cheese. Cook, covered, for 5-10 minutes or until cheese is melted. Top with chips. If desired, serve with sour cream, minced cilantro and additional onion.

NOTES

MOMMA'S TURKEY STEW WITH DUMPLINGS

My mother used to make turkey stew every year with our Thanksgiving leftovers. It's simple and really celebrates the natural flavors of good, simple ingredients. To this day it's one of my favorite meals.

—STEPHANIE RABBITT-SCHAPP CINCINNATI, OH

PREP: 20 MIN. • **COOK:** 6½ HOURS • **MAKES:** 6 SERVINGS

- 3 cups shredded cooked turkey
- 1 large sweet onion, chopped
- 1 large potato, peeled and cubed
- 2 large carrots, chopped
- 2 celery ribs, chopped
- 2 bay leaves
- 1 teaspoon salt
- ½ teaspoon poultry seasoning
- ½ teaspoon dried thyme
- ¼ teaspoon pepper
- 1 carton (32 ounces) chicken broth
- ⅓ cup cold water
- 3 tablespoons cornstarch
- ½ cup frozen corn, thawed
- ½ cup frozen peas, thawed
- 1 cup biscuit/baking mix
- ⅓ cup 2% milk

1. In a 6-qt. slow cooker, combine the first 10 ingredients; stir in broth. Cover and cook on low for 6-7 hours.

2. Remove the bay leaves. In a small bowl, mix water and cornstarch until smooth; stir into the turkey mixture. Add corn and peas. Cover and cook on high until the mixture reaches a simmer.

3. Meanwhile, in a small bowl, mix baking mix and milk just until moistened. Drop by rounded tablespoonfuls on top of the simmering liquid. Reduce heat to low; cover and cook for 20-25 minutes or until a toothpick inserted in a dumpling comes out clean.

SLOW-COOKED TURKEY STROGANOFF

PREP: 20 MIN. • **COOK:** 6 HOURS • **MAKES:** 6 SERVINGS

- **4 turkey thighs (about 4 pounds)**
- **1 large onion, halved and thinly sliced**
- **1 can (10¾ ounces) condensed cream of celery soup, undiluted**
- **⅓ cup water**
- **3 garlic cloves, minced**
- **2 teaspoons dried tarragon**
- **½ teaspoon salt**
- **½ teaspoon pepper**
- **½ cup sour cream**
- **Hot cooked egg noodles**

1. Place turkey and onion in a 5-qt. slow cooker. In a large bowl, whisk soup, water, garlic, tarragon, salt and pepper until blended; pour over top of the turkey. Cook, covered, on low for 6-8 hours or until the meat is tender.

2. Remove the turkey from slow cooker. When cool enough to handle, remove meat from bones; discard bones. Shred the meat with two forks. Whisk sour cream into cooking juices; return the meat to slow cooker. Serve with noodles.

I have been making this tasty dish for 30-plus years. Our family loves turkey, and I make a variety of turkey dishes, but this is our favorite. I love it because I can put it in my slow cooker before I leave for work and come home to a hot, delicious dinner.

—**CINDY ADAMS** TRACY, CA

CHICKEN, SMASHED POTATOES & GRAVY

On chilly days, I crave this yummy chicken with potatoes and gravy. Share it with the family, or take it to potlucks and watch it disappear.

—DEBORAH POSEY

VIRGINIA BEACH, VA

PREP: 30 MIN. • **COOK:** 3 HOURS
MAKES: 6 SERVINGS

- 2 **pounds small red potatoes, quartered**
- 3 **tablespoons water**
- 2 **pounds boneless skinless chicken breasts**
- 1 **medium onion, sliced**
- 2 **medium carrots, cut into 2-inch pieces**
- 2 **celery ribs, cut into 2-inch pieces**
- 3 **garlic cloves, minced**
- 2 **bay leaves**
- 1½ **teaspoons pepper, divided**
- 2½ **cups chicken broth**
- ½ **cup white wine or additional chicken broth**
- 4 **ounces cream cheese, softened**
- ¾ **teaspoon salt, divided**
- 3 **tablespoons butter**
- 3 **tablespoons all-purpose flour**
- ½ **cup 2% milk**
  Minced chives, optional

1. In a large microwave-safe bowl, combine potatoes and water. Microwave, covered, on high for 10-12 minutes or just until tender. Cool slightly; drain.

2. Transfer potatoes to a 5-qt. slow cooker. Add chicken, vegetables, garlic, bay leaves and 1 teaspoon pepper. Pour broth and wine over the chicken and vegetables. Cook, covered, on low for 3-4 hours or until a thermometer reads 165° and the potatoes are tender. Remove chicken from slow cooker; tent with foil.

3. Strain cooking juices, reserving potatoes and cooking juices; discard remaining vegetables and bay leaves. In a large bowl, mash potatoes with cream cheese, ¼ teaspoon salt, ¼ teaspoon pepper and enough cooking juices to reach desired consistency; keep warm

4. In a small saucepan, melt butter over medium heat. Stir in flour until blended; cook and stir 1-2 minutes. Gradually whisk in 1 cup cooking juices, milk and remaining salt and pepper. Bring to a boil, stirring constantly; cook and stir 2-3 minutes or until thickened.

5. Discard the remaining cooking juices. Slice the chicken; serve with potatoes, gravy and, if desired, chives.

PINEAPPLE CHICKEN

PREP: 15 MIN. • **COOK:** 4 HOURS
MAKES: 4 SERVINGS

- **4 bone-in chicken breast halves (12 to 14 ounces each), skin removed**
- **1 tablespoon canola oil**
- **1 can (20 ounces) sliced pineapple**
- **⅓ cup packed brown sugar**
- **¼ cup cornstarch**
- **2 tablespoons lemon juice**
- **¾ teaspoon salt**
- **¼ teaspoon ground ginger**
- **Hot cooked rice**

1. In a large skillet, brown chicken in oil. Transfer to a greased 4-qt. slow cooker. Drain pineapple, reserving juice; place pineapple over the chicken. Whisk brown sugar, cornstarch, lemon juice, salt, ginger and reserved juice until smooth; pour over top.

2. Cover and cook on low 4-5 hours or until chicken is tender. Serve with rice.

> This quick-to-prep recipe tastes a little like sweet-and-sour chicken. It's delicious and perfect for serving with rice.
>
> —FRANCISCA MESIANO
> NEWPORT NEWS, VA

NOTES

LOUISIANA RED BEANS AND RICE

Smoked turkey sausage and red pepper flakes add zip to this slow-cooked version of the New Orleans classic. For extra heat, add red pepper sauce.

—JULIA BUSHREE COMMERCE CITY, CO

PREP: 20 MIN. • **COOK:** 8 HOURS • **MAKES:** 8 SERVINGS

- 4 **cans (16 ounces each) kidney beans, rinsed and drained**
- 1 **can (14½ ounces) diced tomatoes, undrained**
- 1 **package (14 ounces) smoked turkey sausage, sliced**
- 3 **celery ribs, chopped**
- 1 **large onion, chopped**
- 1 **cup chicken broth**
- 1 **medium green pepper, chopped**
- 1 **small sweet red pepper, chopped**
- 6 **garlic cloves, minced**
- 1 **bay leaf**
- ½ **teaspoon crushed red pepper flakes**
- 2 **green onions, chopped**
  Hot cooked rice

1. In a 4- or 5-qt. slow cooker, combine the first 11 ingredients. Cook, covered, on low for 8-10 hours or until the vegetables are tender.

2. Stir before serving. Remove the bay leaf. Serve with green onions and rice.

FREEZE OPTION *Discard bay leaf and freeze cooled bean mixture in freezer containers. To use, partially thaw in refrigerator overnight. Heat through in a saucepan, stirring occasionally and adding a little broth or water if necessary. Serve as directed.*

SLOW COOKER LUAU CHICKEN

PREP: 15 MIN. • **COOK:** 4 HOURS • **MAKES:** 6 SERVINGS

- 6 **bacon strips, divided**
- 6 **boneless skinless chicken thighs (about 1½ pounds)**
- ¼ **teaspoon salt**
- ⅛ **teaspoon pepper**
- ½ **cup chopped red onion**
- 1 **cup crushed pineapple, drained**
- ¾ **cup barbecue sauce**

1. Cut three bacon strips in half; cook until partially cooked but not crisp. Drain on paper towels.

2. Season chicken with salt and pepper; place in a 3-qt. slow cooker. Top each thigh with a half piece of bacon. Top with onion, pineapple and barbecue sauce.

3. Cover and cook on low for 4-5 hours or until the chicken is tender. Cook remaining bacon until crisp; drain and crumble. Sprinkle over each serving.

SLOW COOKER GINGER-PEACH CHICKEN *Omit bacon, salt, pepper, onion, pineapple and barbecue sauce. Place chicken in slow cooker. Top with ¾ cup sliced peeled fresh or thawed frozen peaches and ¾ cup golden raisins. Mix ¾ cup peach preserves, ¼ cup chili sauce, 4 teaspoons minced crystallized ginger, 2 teaspoons minced garlic cloves and 2 teaspoons reduced-sodium soy sauce. Spoon over top. Cook as recipe directs. Serve with hot cooked rice if desired.*

As long as you're cooking bacon for breakfast, save some for the slow cooker. In four short hours, you'll be saying "aloha" to lunch.

—**CINDY LUND** VALLEY CENTER, CA

BUFFALO CHICKEN PASTA

Buffalo chicken is a favorite in our household. Combine it with pasta, and you have the ultimate comfort food. Adding the sour cream, ranch dressing and mozzarella produces a creamy texture that balances the spice.
—**KATHERINE WHITE** CLEMMONS, NC

PREP: 10 MIN. • **COOK:** 4 HOURS • **MAKES:** 8 SERVINGS

- 2 **pounds boneless skinless chicken breasts, cut into 1-inch cubes**
- 2 **cans (10¾ ounces each) condensed cream of chicken soup, undiluted**
- 1 **cup Buffalo wing sauce**
- 1 **medium onion, finely chopped**
- 1½ **teaspoons garlic powder**
- ½ **teaspoon salt**
- ½ **teaspoon pepper**
- 1 **package (16 ounces) penne pasta**
- 2 **cups shredded part-skim mozzarella cheese**
- 2 **cups (16 ounces) sour cream**
- ½ **cup ranch salad dressing**
  Finely chopped celery, optional

1. In a 5-qt. slow cooker, combine the first seven ingredients. Cook, covered, on low for 4-5 hours or until the chicken is tender. Cook pasta according to package directions for al dente; drain.

2. Remove the slow cooker insert. Stir in cheese until melted. Add pasta, sour cream and ranch dressing. If desired, top with celery.

WINE-BRAISED CHICKEN
WITH PEARL ONIONS

PREP: 10 MIN. • **COOK:** 7 HOURS • **MAKES:** 4 SERVINGS

- 8 boneless skinless chicken thighs (about 2 pounds)
- 1 package (14.4 ounces) pearl onions, thawed
- 1 can (10¾ ounces) condensed cream of chicken soup, undiluted
- ¼ cup white wine or chicken broth
- 2 teaspoons minced fresh parsley
- 1 teaspoon dried tarragon
- ½ teaspoon salt
- ¼ teaspoon dried rosemary, crushed
   Hot cooked rice or pasta
   Minced fresh parsley, optional

1. Place chicken and onions in a 4-qt. slow cooker. In a small bowl, combine soup, wine and seasonings; pour over the chicken and onions. Cook, covered, on low for 7-8 hours or until the chicken is tender.

2. Remove the chicken; skim fat from the cooking juices. Serve the cooking juices with the chicken and rice. If desired, sprinkle with parsley.

> This is a family favorite handed down from my grandmother in London. She made it for every family gathering. It was always the first food to go on the table and the first one to disappear.
>
> —**WAYNE E BARNES** MONTGOMERY, AL

SLOW 'N' EASY BARBECUED CHICKEN

I rely on this yummy recipe often during the summer and fall, when I know I'm going to be out working in the yard all day. I just pair it with a side vegetable and salad, and supper is served!

—DREAMA HUGHES LONDON, KY

PREP: 20 MIN. • **COOK:** 3 HOURS • **MAKES:** 4 SERVINGS

- ¼ **cup water**
- 3 **tablespoons brown sugar**
- 3 **tablespoons white vinegar**
- 3 **tablespoons ketchup**
- 2 **tablespoons butter**
- 2 **tablespoons Worcestershire sauce**
- 1 **tablespoon lemon juice**
- 1 **teaspoon salt**
- 1 **teaspoon paprika**
- 1 **teaspoon ground mustard**
- ½ **teaspoon cayenne pepper**
- 1 **broiler/fryer chicken (3 pounds), cut up and skin removed**
- 4 **teaspoons cornstarch**
- 1 **tablespoon cold water**

1. In a small saucepan, combine the first 11 ingredients. Bring to a boil. Reduce heat; simmer, uncovered, for 5 minutes. Remove from the heat.

2. Place chicken in a 3-qt. slow cooker. Top with the sauce. Cover and cook on low for 3-4 hours or until the chicken juices run clear.

3. Remove the chicken to a serving platter; keep warm. Skim the fat from the cooking juices; transfer to a small saucepan. Bring liquid to a boil. Combine cornstarch and water until smooth. Gradually stir into the pan. Bring to a boil; cook and stir for 2 minutes or until thickened. Spoon some of the sauce over the chicken and serve the remaining sauce on the side.

LENTIL & CHICKEN SAUSAGE STEW

PREP: 15 MIN. • **COOK:** 8 HOURS
MAKES: 6 SERVINGS

- 1 **carton (32 ounces) reduced-sodium chicken broth**
- 1 **can (28 ounces) diced tomatoes, undrained**
- 3 **fully cooked spicy chicken sausage links (3 ounces each), cut into ½-inch slices**
- 1 **cup dried lentils, rinsed**
- 1 **medium onion, chopped**
- 1 **medium carrot, chopped**
- 1 **celery rib, chopped**
- 2 **garlic cloves, minced**
- ½ **teaspoon dried thyme**

In a 4- or 5-qt. slow cooker, combine all ingredients. Cover and cook on low for 8-10 hours or until the lentils are tender.

This hearty and healthy stew will warm your family members right down to their toes! Serve with corn bread or rolls to soak up every last morsel.

—**JAN VALDEZ** CHICAGO, IL

SLOW-COOKED CHICKEN A LA KING

When I know I'll be having a busy day with little time to make a meal, I use my slow cooker to prepare this heirloom recipe. It smells so good while it's cooking!

—ELEANOR MIELKE SNOHOMISH, WA

PREP: 10 MIN. • **COOK:** 7½ HOURS • **MAKES:** 6 SERVINGS

- 1 **can (10¾ ounces) reduced-fat reduced-sodium condensed cream of chicken soup, undiluted**
- 3 **tablespoons all-purpose flour**
- ¼ **teaspoon pepper**
  Dash cayenne pepper
- 1 **pound boneless skinless chicken breasts, cubed**
- 1 **celery rib, chopped**
- ½ **cup chopped green pepper**
- ¼ **cup chopped onion**
- 1 **package (10 ounces) frozen peas, thawed**
- 2 **tablespoons diced pimientos, drained**
  Hot cooked rice

In a 3-qt. slow cooker, combine soup, flour, pepper and cayenne until smooth. Stir in chicken, celery, green pepper and onion. Cover and cook on low for 7-8 hours or until the meat juices run clear. Stir in peas and pimientos. Cook 30 minutes longer or until heated through. Serve with rice.

NOTES

OTHER
MAIN DISHES

EYE-OPENING BURRITOS

I use a second slow cooker to keep the tortillas warm when I serve these burritos. Just place a clean wet cloth in the bottom, then cover it with foil and add your tortillas.

—BETH OSBURN LEVELLAND, TX

PREP: 30 MIN. • **COOK:** 4 HOURS
MAKES: 10 SERVINGS

- 1 **pound bulk pork sausage, cooked and drained**
- ½ **pound bacon strips, cooked and crumbled**
- 18 **large eggs, lightly beaten**
- 2 **cups frozen shredded hash brown potatoes, thawed**
- 1 **large onion, chopped**
- 1 **can (10¾ ounces) condensed cheddar cheese soup, undiluted**
- 1 **can (4 ounces) chopped green chilies**
- 1 **teaspoon garlic powder**
- ½ **teaspoon pepper**
- 2 **cups shredded cheddar cheese**
- 10 **flour tortillas (10 inches), warmed**
  Optional toppings: jalapeno peppers, salsa or hot pepper sauce

1. In a large bowl, combine the first nine ingredients. Pour half of the egg mixture into a 4- or 5-qt. slow cooker coated with cooking spray. Top with half of the cheese. Repeat layers.

2. Cook, covered, on low for 4-5 hours or until center is set and a thermometer reads 160°.

3. Spoon ¾ cup of the egg mixture across center of each tortilla. Fold bottom and sides of the tortilla over the filling and roll up. Add toppings of your choice.

SLOW COOKER TUNA NOODLE CASSEROLE

The lemon gives this recipe a nice zip and the potato chips lend a light crunch.

—TASTE OF HOME TEST KITCHEN

PREP: 25 MIN. • **COOK:** 4 HOURS + STANDING
MAKES: 10 SERVINGS

- ¼ **cup butter, cubed**
- ½ **pound sliced fresh mushrooms**
- 1 **medium onion, chopped**
- 1 **medium sweet pepper, chopped**
- 1 **teaspoon salt, divided**
- 1 **teaspoon pepper, divided**
- 2 **garlic cloves, minced**
- ¼ **cup all-purpose flour**
- 2 **cups reduced-sodium chicken broth**
- 2 **cups half-and-half cream**
- 4 **cups uncooked egg noodles (about 6 ounces)**
- 3 **cans (5 ounces each) light tuna in water, drained**
- 2 **tablespoons lemon juice**
- 2 **cups shredded Monterey Jack cheese**
- 2 **cups frozen peas, thawed**
- 2 **cups crushed potato chips**

1. In a large skillet, melt butter over medium-high heat. Add mushrooms, onion, sweet pepper, ½ teaspoon salt and ½ teaspoon pepper; cook and stir 6-8 minutes or until the vegetables are tender. Add garlic; cook 1 minute longer. Stir in flour until blended. Gradually whisk in broth. Bring to a boil, stirring constantly; cook and stir for 1-2 minutes or until thickened.

2. Transfer to a 5-qt. slow cooker. Stir in cream and noodles. Cook, covered, on low for 4-5 hours or until the noodles are tender. Meanwhile, in a small bowl, combine tuna, lemon juice and remaining salt and pepper.

3. Remove the insert from the slow cooker. Stir cheese, tuna mixture and peas into noodle mixture. Let stand, uncovered, 20 minutes. Just before serving, sprinkle with potato chips.

PEACHY BABY BACK RIBS

PREP: 15 MIN. • **COOK:** 6 HOURS • **MAKES:** 6 SERVINGS

- **2 bottles (18 ounces each) hickory smoke-flavored barbecue sauce**
- **1 can (15 ounces) sliced peaches, drained and halved crosswise**
- **1 medium onion, chopped**
- **¾ cup jalapeno pepper jelly**
- **½ cup pickled hot jalapeno slices**
- **6 pounds pork baby back ribs, well-trimmed**
- **1 teaspoon salt**
- **½ teaspoon pepper**
- **Thinly sliced green onions**

1. In a large bowl, mix the first five ingredients. Cut ribs into 3-rib portions; sprinkle with salt and pepper. Place half of the ribs in a 6-qt. slow cooker; pour half of the sauce mixture over the ribs. Repeat layers. Cook, covered, on low for 6-8 hours or until the meat is tender.

2. Remove ribs from slow cooker; keep warm. Strain cooking juices, reserving peaches and vegetables. Skim fat from the cooking juices; thicken if desired. Stir in the reserved peaches and vegetables; serve with ribs. Sprinkle with green onions.

I added sweet peachy flavor and jalapeno heat to classic baby back ribs. All my friends who love barbecue say this is a real winner!

—MARY LOUISE BURK-LEVER ROME, GA

RAISIN NUT OATMEAL

PREP: 10 MIN. • **COOK:** 7 HOURS
MAKES: 6 SERVINGS

- 3½ cups fat-free milk
- 1 large apple, peeled and chopped
- ¾ cup steel-cut oats
- ¾ cup raisins
- 3 tablespoons brown sugar
- 4½ teaspoons butter, melted
- ¾ teaspoon ground cinnamon
- ½ teaspoon salt
- ¼ cup chopped pecans

In a 3-qt. slow cooker coated with cooking spray, combine the first eight ingredients. Cover and cook on low for 7-8 hours or until liquid is absorbed. Spoon oatmeal into bowls; sprinkle with pecans.

NOTE *You may substitute 1½ cups quick-cooking oats for the steel-cut oats and increase the fat-free milk to 4½ cups.*

There's no better feeling than waking up to a hot, ready-to-eat breakfast. The oats, fruit and spices in this homey meal cook together while you sleep.

—**VALERIE SAUBER** ADELANTO, CA

SOUTHERN LOADED SWEET POTATOES

For a taste of a real Southern classic, we make sweet potatoes stuffed with pulled pork and coleslaw, and manage to sidestep the calorie overload.

—AMY BURTON FUQUAY VARINA, NC

PREP: 15 MIN. • **COOK:** 6 HOURS • **MAKES:** 8 SERVINGS

- 1 **boneless pork loin roast (2 to 3 pounds)**
- ½ **cup Dijon mustard, divided**
- 1 **tablespoon brown sugar**
- 1 **tablespoon garlic powder**
- 1 **teaspoon cayenne pepper**
- 1 **teaspoon salt, divided**
- 1 **cup reduced-sodium beef broth**
- 8 **medium sweet potatoes (about 5 pounds)**
- 3 **cups coleslaw mix**
- ½ **cup fat-free plain Greek yogurt**
- ½ **cup reduced-fat mayonnaise**
- 2 **tablespoons cider vinegar**
- ½ **teaspoon celery seed**
- ¼ **teaspoon garlic salt**

1. Place pork roast in a 3-qt. slow cooker. In a small bowl, mix ⅓ cup mustard, brown sugar, garlic powder, cayenne and ½ teaspoon salt; brush over the pork. Add broth; cook, covered, on low for 6-8 hours or until the meat is tender.

2. Meanwhile, preheat oven to 400°. Scrub potatoes; pierce several times with a fork. Bake 45-50 minutes or until tender.

3. Place coleslaw mix in a large bowl. In a small bowl, whisk yogurt, mayonnaise, vinegar, celery seed, garlic salt and remaining mustard and salt; pour over the coleslaw mix and toss to coat.

4. Remove the roast; cool slightly. Shred the pork with two forks; return meat to slow cooker.

5. With a sharp knife, cut an "X" in each potato. Fluff the pulp with a fork. Using a slotted spoon, place pork mixture and coleslaw over each potato.

FORGOTTEN JAMBALAYA

During the chilly seasons, I fix this jambalaya at least once a month. It's so easy—just chop the vegetables, dump everything in the slow cooker and forget it. Even my sons, who are picky about spicy foods, like this dish.
—CINDI COSS COPPELL, TX

PREP: 35 MIN. • **COOK:** 4¼ HOURS
MAKES: 11 SERVINGS

- 1 can (14½ ounces) diced tomatoes, undrained
- 1 can (14½ ounces) beef or chicken broth
- 1 can (6 ounces) tomato paste
- 3 celery ribs, chopped
- 2 medium green peppers, chopped
- 1 medium onion, chopped
- 5 garlic cloves, minced
- 3 teaspoons dried parsley flakes
- 2 teaspoons dried basil
- 1½ teaspoons dried oregano
- 1¼ teaspoons salt
- ½ teaspoon cayenne pepper
- ½ teaspoon hot pepper sauce
- 1 pound boneless skinless chicken breasts, cut into 1-inch cubes
- 1 pound smoked sausage, halved and cut into ¼-inch slices
- ½ pound uncooked medium shrimp, peeled and deveined
  Hot cooked rice

1. In a 5-qt. slow cooker, combine tomatoes, broth and tomato paste. Stir in celery, green peppers, onion, garlic and seasonings. Stir in chicken and sausage.

2. Cover and cook on low 4-6 hours or until the chicken is no longer pink. Stir in shrimp. Cover and cook 15-30 minutes longer or until the shrimp turn pink. Serve with rice.

FREEZE OPTION *Place individual portions of cooled stew in freezer containers and freeze. To use, partially thaw in refrigerator overnight. Heat stew through in a saucepan, stirring occasionally and adding a little water if necessary.*

HAM WITH PINEAPPLE SAUCE

PREP: 10 MIN. • **COOK:** 6 HOURS
MAKES: 12 SERVINGS

- 1 **fully cooked boneless ham
  (4 to 5 pounds)**
- 1 **can (20 ounces) unsweetened
  crushed pineapple, undrained**
- 1 **cup packed brown sugar**
- 1 **tablespoon cornstarch**
- ¼ **teaspoon salt**
- 2 **tablespoons lemon juice**
- 1 **tablespoon yellow mustard**

Place ham in a 5-qt. slow cooker. In a small saucepan, mix the remaining ingredients, stirring to dissolve cornstarch. Bring to a boil, stirring occasionally. Pour over the ham, covering completely. Cover and cook on low for 6-8 hours.
NOTE *This recipe is not recommended for a spiral-cut ham.*

Although we serve this dish for special occasions, it makes it to the table all year round. It's so simple to prepare, and everyone goes crazy for it.

—TERRY ROBERTS YORKTOWN, VA

SPICY LENTIL & CHICKPEA STEW

This recipe came to me from a friend. I changed a few things until I found a version that my family loves. My 5-year-old son doesn't like things too spicy, so I make the stew milder for him. My husband works outdoors for long hours at a time and finds this soup hearty enough to keep him satisfied.

—MELANIE MACFARLANE BEDEQUE, PE

PREP: 25 MIN. • **COOK:** 8 HOURS • **MAKES:** 8 SERVINGS (2¾ QUARTS)

- 2 teaspoons olive oil
- 1 medium onion, thinly sliced
- 1 teaspoon dried oregano
- ½ teaspoon crushed red pepper flakes
- 2 cans (15 ounces each) chickpeas, rinsed and drained
- 1 cup dried lentils, rinsed
- 1 can (2¼ ounces) sliced ripe olives, drained
- 3 teaspoons smoked paprika
- 4 cups vegetable broth
- 4 cans (8 ounces each) no-salt-added tomato sauce
- 4 cups fresh baby spinach
- ¾ cup fat-free plain yogurt

1. In a small skillet, heat oil over medium-high heat. Add onion, oregano and pepper flakes; cook and stir for 8-10 minutes or until the onion is tender. Transfer to a 5- or 6-qt. slow cooker.

2. Add chickpeas, lentils, olives and paprika; stir in broth and tomato sauce. Cook, covered, on low for 8-10 hours or until the lentils are tender. Stir in spinach. Top individual servings with yogurt.

NOTES

CREAMY CURRY VEGETABLE STEW

Our family loves to eat Indian food, and this recipe is quick and easy to make with jarred korma sauce and fresh spring vegetables. If you want a hotter dish, add cayenne pepper to taste. Sometimes I add grilled chicken to the recipe. I serve this with naan bread, chutney and flaked coconut for condiments. So good!

—NANCY HEISHMAN LAS VEGAS, NV

PREP: 25 MIN. • **COOK:** 7 HOURS • **MAKES:** 6 SERVINGS

- 2 jars (15 ounces each) korma curry sauce
- 2 tablespoons curry powder
- 2 teaspoons garam masala
- 1½ teaspoons ground mustard
- 2 pounds red potatoes (about 6 medium), cubed
- 2 cups small fresh mushrooms
- 2 cups fresh baby carrots
- 1½ cups frozen corn, thawed
- 5 green onions, chopped
- 2 cups cut fresh asparagus (2-inch pieces)
- 2 tablespoons water
- 1½ cups frozen peas, thawed
- ¼ cup chopped fresh parsley
  Naan flatbreads or cooked basmati rice, optional

1. In a greased 5-qt. slow cooker, combine curry sauce, curry powder, garam masala and mustard. Stir in potatoes, mushrooms, carrots, corn and green onions. Cook, covered, on low for 7-9 hours or until the vegetables are tender.

2. In a microwave-safe bowl, combine asparagus and water; microwave, covered, on high for 2-3 minutes or until crisp-tender. Drain. Stir the asparagus and peas into slow cooker; heat through. Sprinkle with parsley. If desired, serve with naan or basmati rice.

NOTE *Look for garam masala in the spice aisle.*

SAUSAGE SAUERKRAUT SUPPER

PREP: 25 MIN. • **COOK:** 8 HOURS • **MAKES:** 10-12 SERVINGS

- 4 **cups carrot chunks (2-inch pieces)**
- 4 **cups red potato chunks**
- 2 **cans (14 ounces each) sauerkraut, rinsed and drained**
- 2½ **pounds fresh Polish sausage links**
- 1 **medium onion, thinly sliced**
- 3 **garlic cloves, minced**
- 1½ **cups dry white wine or chicken broth**
- 1 **teaspoon pepper**
- ½ **teaspoon caraway seeds**

1. In a 5-qt. slow cooker, layer the carrots, potatoes and sauerkraut. In a large skillet, brown sausages. When cool enough to handle, cut the sausages into 3-inch pieces; transfer to slow cooker (slow cooker will be full). Reserve 1 tablespoon drippings; saute onion and garlic in reserved drippings until tender.

2. Gradually add wine to the skillet. Bring to a boil; stir to loosen browned bits. Stir in pepper and caraway. Pour over sausage. Cover and cook on low for 8-10 hours or until a thermometer inserted in the sausage reads 160°.

With big, tender chunks of sausage, potatoes and carrots, this meal-in-one has old-world flavor that will satisfy even the heartiest of appetites. It always disappears in a hurry when served at a family gathering or office potluck.

—**JOALYCE GRAHAM** ST. PETERSBURG, FL

SAUSAGE, ARTICHOKE &
SUN-DRIED TOMATO RAGU

Don't be intimidated by the number of ingredients for this recipe. The hardest part will be waiting for the dish to be done so you can devour it.

—AYSHA SCHURMAN AMMON, ID

PREP: 20 MIN. • **COOK:** 6 HOURS • **MAKES:** 2 QUARTS

- 1 pound bulk Italian sausage
- ½ pound lean ground beef (90% lean)
- 1 medium onion, finely chopped
- 3 cans (14½ ounces each) diced tomatoes, undrained
- 1 cup oil-packed sun-dried tomatoes, chopped
- 2 cans (6 ounces each) Italian tomato paste
- 1 jar (7½ ounces) marinated quartered artichoke hearts, drained and chopped
- 3 garlic cloves, minced
- 2 teaspoons minced fresh rosemary
- 1 teaspoon pepper
- ½ teaspoon salt
- 1 bay leaf
- 3 tablespoons minced fresh parsley
   Hot cooked spaghetti
   Grated Parmesan cheese, optional

1. In a large skillet, cook sausage, beef and onion over medium-high heat for 4-6 minutes or until the meat is no longer pink, breaking into crumbles; drain. Transfer to a 5- or 6-qt. slow cooker. Stir in tomatoes, tomato paste, artichokes, garlic, rosemary, pepper, salt and bay leaf.

2. Cook, covered, on low for 6-8 hours or until heated through. Remove the bay leaf. Stir in parsley. Serve with spaghetti. If desired, top with grated Parmesan.

FREEZE OPTION *Freeze cooled sauce in freezer containers. To use, partially thaw in refrigerator overnight. Heat through in a saucepan, stirring occasionally.*

EASY CHILI VERDE

PREP: 10 MIN. • **COOK:** 5 HOURS
MAKES: 12 SERVINGS (3 QUARTS)

- **1 boneless pork shoulder roast (4 to 5 pounds), cut into 1-inch pieces**
- **3 cans (10 ounces each) green enchilada sauce**
- **1 cup salsa verde**
- **1 can (4 ounces) chopped green chilies**
- **½ teaspoon salt**
  Hot cooked rice
  Sour cream, optional

In a 5-qt. slow cooker, combine pork, enchilada sauce, salsa verde, green chilies and salt. Cook, covered, on low for 5-6 hours or until the pork is tender. Serve with rice. If desired, top with sour cream.

I love chili verde and order it whenever I can at restaurants. A few years ago I figured out how to make an easy, tasty version at home. There are never leftovers when I make it. Sprinkle with fresh cilantro and lime juice for brighter flavor.

—JULIE ROWLAND SALT LAKE CITY, UT

HELPFUL HINT

You don't have to serve this recipe as a salad—warm up some tortillas, fill them with the richly spiced shredded pork, and layer the greens, vegetables and cheese on top!

SOUTHWEST SHREDDED PORK SALAD

This knockout shredded pork makes a healthy, delicious and hearty salad with black beans, corn, cotija cheese and plenty of fresh greens.

—MARY SHIVERS ADA, OK

PREP: 20 MIN. • **COOK:** 6 HOURS • **MAKES:** 12 SERVINGS

- 1 boneless pork loin roast (3 to 4 pounds)
- 1½ cups apple cider or juice
- 1 can (4 ounces) chopped green chilies, drained
- 3 garlic cloves, minced
- 1½ teaspoons salt
- 1½ teaspoons hot pepper sauce
- 1 teaspoon chili powder
- 1 teaspoon pepper
- ½ teaspoon ground cumin
- ½ teaspoon dried oregano
- 12 cups torn mixed salad greens
- 1 can (15 ounces) black beans, rinsed and drained
- 2 medium tomatoes, chopped
- 1 small red onion, chopped
- 1 cup fresh or frozen (thawed) corn
- 1 cup crumbled cotija or shredded part-skim mozzarella cheese
  Salad dressing of your choice

1. Place pork in a 5- or 6-qt. slow cooker. In a small bowl, mix cider, green chilies, garlic, salt, pepper sauce, chili powder, pepper, cumin and oregano; pour over the pork. Cook, covered, on low for 6-8 hours or until the meat is tender.

2. Remove roast from slow cooker; discard the cooking juices. Shred the pork with two forks. Arrange salad greens on a large serving platter. Top with pork, black beans, tomatoes, onion, corn and cheese. Serve with salad dressing.

FREEZE OPTION *Place shredded pork in a freezer container; top with cooking juices. Cool and freeze. To use, partially thaw in refrigerator overnight. Heat through in a saucepan, stirring occasionally.*

TERIYAKI PORK ROAST

PREP: 10 MIN. • **COOK:** 7 HOURS
MAKES: 8 SERVINGS

- ¾ cup unsweetened apple juice
- 2 tablespoons sugar
- 2 tablespoons reduced-sodium soy sauce
- 1 tablespoon white vinegar
- 1 teaspoon ground ginger
- ¼ teaspoon garlic powder
- ⅛ teaspoon pepper
- 1 boneless pork loin roast (about 3 pounds), halved
- 7½ teaspoons cornstarch
- 3 tablespoons cold water

1. In a greased 3-qt. slow cooker, combine the first seven ingredients. Add roast and turn to coat. Cover and cook on low for 7-8 hours or until the meat is tender.

2. Remove the pork to a serving platter; keep warm. Skim fat from the cooking juices; transfer to a small saucepan. Bring liquid to a boil. Combine cornstarch and water until smooth. Gradually stir into the pan. Bring to a boil; cook and stir for 2 minutes or until thickened. Serve with the meat.

I'm always looking for no-fuss recipes, so I was thrilled to find this one. The tender teriyaki pork has become a family favorite.

—**ROXANNE HULSEY** GAINESVILLE, GA

SLOW COOKER CHORIZO BREAKFAST CASSEROLE

My kids ask for this slow-cooked casserole for breakfast and dinner. I've served it with white country gravy and with salsa—it's delightful either way.

—CINDY PRUITT GROVE, OK

PREP: 25 MIN. • **COOK:** 4 HOURS + STANDING
MAKES: 8 SERVINGS

- 1 **pound fresh chorizo or bulk spicy pork sausage**
- 1 **medium onion, chopped**
- 1 **medium sweet red pepper, chopped**
- 2 **jalapeno peppers, seeded and chopped**
- 1 **package (30 ounces) frozen shredded hash brown potatoes, thawed**
- 1½ **cups shredded Mexican cheese blend**
- 12 **large eggs**
- 1 **cup 2% milk**
- ½ **teaspoon pepper**

1. In a large skillet, cook chorizo, onion, red pepper and jalapenos over medium heat for 7-8 minutes or until the chorizo is cooked through and the vegetables are tender, breaking chorizo into crumbles; drain. Cool slightly.

2. In a greased 5-qt. slow cooker, layer a third of the potatoes, chorizo mixture and cheese. Repeat layers twice. In a large bowl, whisk the eggs, milk and pepper until blended; pour over top.

3. Cook, covered, on low for 4-4½ hours or until the eggs are set and a thermometer reads 160°. Uncover and let stand 10 minutes before serving.

NOTE *Wear disposable gloves when cutting hot peppers; the oils can burn skin. Avoid touching your face.*

SAUSAGE WITH JALAPENO POTATOES

This flavor-packed recipe stands out from your typical sausage dish.
—ROSE SMITH ROYALTON, IL

PREP: 25 MIN. • **COOK:** 5 HOURS • **MAKES:** 6 SERVINGS

- 3 **pounds potatoes (about 6 medium), peeled and cut into 1-inch cubes**
- 3 **jalapeno peppers, seeded and sliced**
- ¼ **cup butter, cubed**
- 2 **tablespoons water**
- 3 **garlic cloves, minced**
- ¾ **teaspoon salt**
- ¼ **teaspoon pepper**
- 2 **medium sweet red peppers, halved and cut into 1-inch strips**
- 2 **medium sweet yellow or orange peppers, halved and cut into 1-inch strips**
- 1 **large onion, halved and thinly sliced**
- 1 **teaspoon olive oil**
- 5 **Italian sausage links (4 ounces each)**
  Chopped fresh basil, optional

1. Place the first seven ingredients in a 6-qt. slow cooker; toss to combine. Top with sweet peppers and onion.

2. In a large skillet, heat oil over medium-high heat. Brown sausages on all sides; place over the vegetables. Cook, covered, on low for 5-6 hours or until the potatoes are tender.

3. Remove the sausages; cut diagonally into 2- to 3-in. pieces. Remove the vegetables with a slotted spoon; serve with the sausage. If desired, sprinkle with basil.

NOTE *Wear disposable gloves when cutting hot peppers; the oils can burn skin. Avoid touching your face.*

LIP SMACKIN' RIBS

PREP: 20 MIN. • **COOK:** 6 HOURS
MAKES: 8 SERVINGS

- 3 **tablespoons butter**
- 3 **pounds boneless country-style pork ribs**
- 1 **can (15 ounces) tomato sauce**
- 1 **cup packed brown sugar**
- 1 **cup ketchup**
- ¼ **cup prepared mustard**
- 2 **tablespoons honey**
- 3 **teaspoons pepper**
- 2 **teaspoons dried savory**
- 1 **teaspoon salt**

In a large skillet, heat butter over medium heat. Brown ribs in batches; transfer to a 5-qt. slow cooker. Add the remaining ingredients. Cook, covered, on low for 6-8 hours or until the meat is tender.

No matter what time of year you eat them, these ribs taste like summer. They're a feel-good food!

—**RON BYNAKER** LEBANON, PA

SNACKS &
SWEETS

SLOW-COOKED SALSA

I love the fresh taste of homemade salsa, but as a working mother, I don't have much time to make it. So I came up with this slow-cooked version that practically makes itself!
—TONI MENARD LOMPOC, CA

PREP: 15 MIN. • **COOK:** 2½ HOURS + COOLING
MAKES: ABOUT 2 CUPS

- 10 **plum tomatoes**
- 2 **garlic cloves**
- 1 **small onion, cut into wedges**
- 2 **jalapeno peppers**
- ¼ **cup cilantro leaves**
- ½ **teaspoon salt, optional**

1. Core tomatoes. Cut a small slit in two tomatoes; insert a garlic clove into each slit. Place the tomatoes and onion in a 3-qt. slow cooker.
2. Cut stems off jalapenos; remove seeds if a milder salsa is desired. Place jalapenos in the slow cooker.
3. Cover and cook on high for 2½-3 hours or until the vegetables are softened (some may brown slightly); cool.
4. In a blender, combine the tomato mixture, cilantro and, if desired, salt; cover and process until blended. Refrigerate the leftovers.

NOTE *Wear disposable gloves when cutting hot peppers; the oils can burn skin. Avoid touching your face.*

MARMALADE MEATBALLS

PREP: 10 MIN. • **COOK:** 4 HOURS • **MAKES:** ABOUT 5 DOZEN

- 1 **bottle (16 ounces) Catalina salad dressing**
- 1 **cup orange marmalade**
- 3 **tablespoons Worcestershire sauce**
- ½ **teaspoon crushed red pepper flakes**
- 1 **package (32 ounces) frozen fully cooked home-style meatballs, thawed**

In a 3-qt. slow cooker, combine salad dressing, marmalade, Worcestershire sauce and pepper flakes. Stir in meatballs. Cover and cook on low for 4-5 hours or until heated through.

FREEZE OPTION *Freeze cooled meatball mixture in freezer containers. To use, partially thaw in refrigerator overnight. Microwave, covered, on high in a microwave-safe dish until heated through, gently stirring and adding a little water if necessary.*

EASY PARTY MEATBALLS *Omit first four ingredients. Combine 1 bottle (14 ounces) ketchup, ¼ cup A.1. steak sauce, 1 tablespoon minced garlic and 1 teaspoon Dijon mustard in slow cooker; stir in meatballs. Cook as directed.*

I brought this snappy recipe to work for a potluck. I started cooking the meatballs in the morning, and by lunchtime they were ready. They disappeared fast!

—**JEANNE KISS** GREENSBURG, PA

HELPFUL HINT

Slow cookers vary, so refer to the manual provided by the manufacturer. But in general, set your slow cooker at "low" for 200° and "high" for 300°.

BBQ CHICKEN SLIDERS

Brining chicken overnight helps it taste exceptionally good, making it so tender it literally melts in your mouth.
—RACHEL KUNKEL SCHELL CITY, MO

PREP: 25 MIN. + BRINING • **COOK:** 4 HOURS
MAKES: 8 SERVINGS (2 SLIDERS EACH)

BRINE
- 1½ **quarts water**
- ¼ **cup packed brown sugar**
- 2 **tablespoons salt**
- 1 **tablespoon liquid smoke**
- 2 **garlic cloves, minced**
- ½ **teaspoon dried thyme**

CHICKEN
- 2 **pounds boneless skinless chicken breast halves**
- ⅓ **cup liquid smoke**
- 1½ **cups hickory smoke-flavored barbecue sauce**
- 16 **slider buns or dinner rolls, split and warmed**

1. In a large bowl, mix brine ingredients, stirring to dissolve brown sugar. Reserve 1 cup brine for cooking chicken; cover and refrigerate.

2. Place chicken in a large resealable bag; add remaining brine. Seal bag, pressing out as much air as possible; turn to coat the chicken. Place in a large bowl; refrigerate for 18-24 hours, turning occasionally.

3. Remove chicken from brine and transfer to a 3-qt. slow cooker; discard brine in bag. Add reserved 1 cup brine and ⅓ cup liquid smoke to chicken. Cook, covered, on low for 4-5 hours or until the chicken is tender.

4. Remove chicken; cool slightly. Discard cooking juices. Shred the chicken with two forks and return to the slow cooker. Stir in barbecue sauce; heat through. Serve on buns.

CHAMPIONSHIP BEAN DIP

PREP: 10 MIN. • **COOK:** 2 HOURS
MAKES: 4½ CUPS

- **1 can (16 ounces) refried beans**
- **1 cup picante sauce**
- **1 cup shredded Monterey Jack cheese**
- **1 cup shredded cheddar cheese**
- **¾ cup sour cream**
- **1 package (3 ounces) cream cheese, softened**
- **1 tablespoon chili powder**
- **¼ teaspoon ground cumin**
  Tortilla chips and salsa

In a large bowl, combine the first eight ingredients; transfer to a 1½-qt. slow cooker. Cover and cook on high for 2 hours or until heated through, stirring once or twice. Serve with tortilla chips and salsa.

My friends and neighbors expect me to bring this irresistible dip to every gathering. When I arrive they ask if I brought my bean dip. If there are any leftovers, we use them to make bean and cheese burritos the next day.

—**WENDI WAVRIN LAW** OMAHA, NE

CHERRY COLA CHOCOLATE CAKE

This easy dessert comes out warm, moist, fudgy and wonderful. And it won't heat up the entire kitchen.

—ELAINE SWEET DALLAS, TX

PREP: 30 MIN. + STANDING • **COOK:** 2 HOURS + STANDING
MAKES: 8 SERVINGS

- ½ cup cola
- ½ cup dried tart cherries
- 1½ cups all-purpose flour
- ½ cup sugar
- 2 ounces semisweet chocolate, chopped
- 2½ teaspoons baking powder
- ½ teaspoon salt
- 1 cup chocolate milk
- ½ cup butter, melted
- 2 teaspoons vanilla extract

TOPPING

- 1¼ cups cola
- ½ cup sugar
- ½ cup packed brown sugar
- 2 ounces semisweet chocolate, chopped
- ¼ cup dark rum
  Vanilla ice cream and maraschino cherries, optional

1. In a small saucepan, bring cola and dried cherries to a boil. Remove from heat; let stand for 30 minutes.

2. In a large bowl, combine flour, sugar, chocolate, baking powder and salt. Combine chocolate milk, butter and vanilla; stir into the dry ingredients just until moistened. Fold in the cherry mixture. Pour into a 3-qt. slow cooker coated with cooking spray.

3. For topping, in a small saucepan, combine cola, sugar and brown sugar. Cook and stir until the sugar is dissolved. Remove from heat; stir in chocolate and rum until smooth. Pour over the batter; do not stir.

4. Cover and cook on high for 2-2½ hours or until set. Turn off heat; let stand, covered, for 30 minutes. Serve warm with ice cream and maraschino cherries if desired.

BRISKET SLIDERS WITH CARAMELIZED ONIONS

For a dear friend's going-away party, I made a juicy brisket and turned it into sliders. Cook the brisket ahead and the slider assembly will be a breeze.

—MARLIES COVENTRY
NORTH VANCOUVER, BC

PREP: 25 MIN. + MARINATING
COOK: 7 HOURS • **MAKES:** 2 DOZEN

- 2 **tablespoons plus ⅛ teaspoon salt, divided**
- 2 **tablespoons sugar**
- 2 **tablespoons whole peppercorns, crushed**
- 5 **garlic cloves, minced**
- 1 **fresh beef brisket (about 4 pounds)**
- 1 **cup mayonnaise**
- ½ **cup crumbled blue cheese**
- 2 **teaspoons horseradish**
- ⅛ **teaspoon cayenne pepper**
- 3 **medium carrots, cut into 1-inch pieces**
- 2 **medium onions, chopped**
- 2 **celery ribs, chopped**
- 1 **cup dry red wine or beef broth**
- ¼ **cup stone-ground mustard**
- 3 **bay leaves**
- 1 **tablespoon olive oil**
- 3 **medium onions, sliced**
- 24 **mini buns**
  Arugula and tomato slices, optional

1. Combine 2 tablespoons salt, sugar, peppercorns and garlic; rub onto all sides of brisket. Wrap in plastic and refrigerate 8 hours or overnight. In a small bowl, combine mayonnaise, blue cheese, horseradish and cayenne pepper. Refrigerate until assembling.

2. Place carrots, chopped onions and celery in a 6- or 7-qt. slow cooker. Unwrap the brisket; place on top of the vegetables. In a small bowl, combine red wine, mustard and bay leaves; pour over the brisket. Cook, covered, on low for 7-9 hours or until the meat is fork-tender. Meanwhile, in a large skillet, heat oil over medium heat. Add sliced onions and the remaining salt; cook and stir until softened. Reduce heat to medium-low; cook for 30-35 minutes or until the onions are deep golden brown, stirring occasionally.

3. Remove the brisket; cool slightly. Reserve 1 cup cooking juices; discard the remaining juices. Skim fat from reserved juices. Thinly slice brisket across the grain; return to the slow cooker. Pour juices over brisket.

4. Serve brisket on buns with the mayonnaise mixture and caramelized onions and, if desired, arugula and tomato slices.

HELPFUL HINT

You can caramelize the onions a day in advance. Cool, cover and refrigerate. The next day, reheat the onions and serve with the slow-cooked brisket.

PADDY'S REUBEN DIP

This slow-cooked spread tastes just like the popular Reuben sandwich. Even when I double the recipe, I end up with an empty dish.

—MARY JANE KIMMES HASTINGS, MN

PREP: 5 MIN. • **COOK:** 2 HOURS • **MAKES:** ABOUT 4 CUPS

- **4 packages (2 ounces each) thinly sliced deli corned beef, finely chopped**
- **1 package (8 ounces) cream cheese, cubed**
- **1 can (8 ounces) sauerkraut, rinsed and drained**
- **1 cup (8 ounces) sour cream**
- **1 cup shredded Swiss cheese**
  Rye bread or crackers

In a 1½-qt. slow cooker, combine the first five ingredients. Cover and cook on low for 2 hours or until the cheese is melted; stir until blended. Serve warm with bread or crackers.

NOTES

HEARTY PORK & BLACK BEAN NACHOS

PREP: 15 MIN. • **COOK:** 6 HOURS • **MAKES:** 10 SERVINGS

- **1 package (4 ounces) beef jerky**
- **3 pounds pork spareribs, cut into 2-rib sections**
- **4 cans (15 ounces each) black beans, rinsed and drained**
- **4 cups beef broth**
- **1 medium onion, chopped**
- **6 bacon strips, cooked and crumbled**
- **3 large garlic cloves, minced**
- **1 teaspoon crushed red pepper flakes**
- **Tortilla chips**
- **Optional toppings: shredded cheddar cheese, sour cream, thinly sliced green onions, pickled jalapenos and chopped tomatoes**

1. Place beef jerky in a food processor; pulse until finely ground. Place ribs in a 5- or 6-qt. slow cooker; top with jerky, beans, broth, onion, bacon, garlic and pepper flakes. Cook, covered, on low for 6-8 hours or until the meat is tender.

2. When cool enough to handle, remove meat from bones; discard bones. Shred meat with two forks; return to slow cooker. Strain pork mixture; discard juices. Serve with chips and toppings as desired.

FREEZE OPTION *Freeze cooled shredded meat mixture with juices in freezer containers. To use, partially thaw in refrigerator overnight. Heat through in a saucepan, stirring occasionally. Strain pork mixture; discard juices. Serve with chips and toppings as desired.*

My husband and I are both graduate students, so we don't have a lot of time to cook dinner. Our family loves coming home to this incredible nacho platter, and I love how easy it is to prepare.

—**FAITH STOKES** CHICKAMAUGA, GA

CHOCOLATY PEANUT CLUSTERS

I turn to my slow cooker to prepare these convenient chocolate treats. Making candies couldn't be any easier!

—PAM POSEY WATERLOO, SC

PREP: 25 MIN. • **COOK:** 2 HOURS + STANDING
MAKES: 6½ POUNDS

- 1 **jar (16 ounces) salted dry roasted peanuts**
- 1 **jar (16 ounces) unsalted dry roasted peanuts**
- 1 **package (11½ ounces) milk chocolate chips**
- 1 **package (10 ounces) peanut butter chips**
- 3 **packages (10 to 12 ounces each) white baking chips**
- 2 **packages (10 ounces each) 60% cacao bittersweet chocolate baking chips**

1. In a 6-qt. slow cooker, combine salted and unsalted peanuts. Layer with the remaining ingredients in order given (do not stir). Cover and cook on low for 2-2½ hours or until the chips are melted, stirring halfway through cooking.
2. Stir to combine. Drop mixture by tablespoonfuls onto waxed paper, then refrigerate until set. Store in an airtight container at room temperature.

CHILI CHEESE AND BEEF DIP

After trying to create a Mexican soup, I wound up with this outstanding dip. My husband and two young children love it for football game days and family gatherings.
—SANDRA FICK LINCOLN, NE

PREP: 20 MIN. • **COOK:** 4½ HOURS • **MAKES:** 8 CUPS

- 1 **pound lean ground beef (90% lean)**
- 1 **medium onion, chopped**
- 1 **can (16 ounces) kidney beans, rinsed and drained**
- 1 **can (15 ounces) black beans, rinsed and drained**
- 1 **can (14½ ounces) diced tomatoes in sauce, undrained**
- 1 **cup frozen corn, thawed**
- ¾ **cup water**
- 1 **can (2¼ ounces) sliced ripe olives, drained**
- 3 **teaspoons chili powder**
- ½ **teaspoon dried oregano**
- ½ **teaspoon chipotle hot pepper sauce**
- ¼ **teaspoon garlic powder**
- ¼ **teaspoon ground cumin**
- 1 **package (16 ounces) reduced-fat process cheese (Velveeta), cubed**
  Corn chips or tortilla chips

1. In a large skillet, cook beef and onion over medium heat for 6-8 minutes or until the beef is no longer pink and the onion is tender, breaking up beef into crumbles; drain. Transfer to a 4-qt. slow cooker.

2. Stir in beans, tomatoes, corn, water, olives, chili powder, oregano, pepper sauce, garlic powder and cumin. Cook, covered, on low for 4-5 hours or until heated through.

3. Stir in process cheese. Cook, covered, on low 30 minutes longer or until the cheese is melted. Serve with corn chips.

SLOW COOKER SPICED MIXED NUTS

PREP: 15 MIN. • **COOK:** 1 HOUR 50 MIN. + COOLING
MAKES: 6 CUPS

- 1 **large egg white**
- 2 **teaspoons vanilla extract**
- 1 **cup unblanched almonds**
- 1 **cup pecan halves**
- 1 **cup shelled walnuts**
- 1 **cup unsalted cashews**
- 1 **cup sugar**
- 1 **cup packed brown sugar**
- 4 **teaspoons ground cinnamon**
- 2 **teaspoons ground ginger**
- 1 **teaspoon ground nutmeg**
- ½ **teaspoon ground cloves**
- ⅛ **teaspoon salt**
- 2 **tablespoons water**

1. In a large bowl, whisk egg white and vanilla until blended; stir in nuts. In a small bowl, mix sugars, spices and salt. Add to the nut mixture and toss to coat.
2. Transfer to a greased 3-qt. slow cooker. Cook, covered, on high for 1½ hours, stirring every 15 minutes. Gradually stir in water. Cook, covered, on low for 20 minutes.
3. Spread onto waxed paper; cool completely. Store in airtight containers up to 1 week.

Just as slow cookers do for soups and stews, they'll do for mixed nuts, too. Just add, stir and enjoy the scent of cooking spices.
—**STEPHANIE LOAIZA** LAYTON, UT

FIVE-CHEESE SPINACH & ARTICHOKE DIP

This is the dish I am always asked to bring to events. I have made it for weddings, Christmas parties and more. Alternatively, this can be baked in the oven at about 400° for 30 minutes or until hot and bubbly.

—NOELLE MYERS GRAND FORKS, ND

PREP: 20 MIN. • **COOK:** 2½ HOURS
MAKES: 16 SERVINGS (¼ CUP EACH)

- 1 jar (12 ounces) roasted sweet red peppers
- 1 jar (6½ ounces) marinated quartered artichoke hearts
- 1 package (10 ounces) frozen chopped spinach, thawed and squeezed dry
- 8 ounces fresh mozzarella cheese, cubed
- 1½ cups shredded Asiago cheese
- 6 ounces cream cheese, softened and cubed
- 1 cup crumbled feta cheese
- ⅓ cup shredded provolone cheese
- ⅓ cup minced fresh basil
- ¼ cup finely chopped red onion
- 2 tablespoons mayonnaise
- 2 garlic cloves, minced
  Assorted crackers

1. Drain peppers, reserving 1 tablespoon liquid; chop the peppers. Drain artichokes, reserving 2 tablespoons liquid; coarsely chop the artichokes.

2. In a 3-qt. slow cooker coated with cooking spray, combine spinach, cheeses, basil, onion, mayonnaise, garlic, artichoke hearts and peppers. Stir in reserved pepper and artichoke liquids. Cook, covered, on high for 2 hours. Stir dip; cook, covered, for 30-60 minutes longer or until the cheese is melted. Stir before serving; serve with crackers.

HELPFUL HINT

Thaw frozen ingredients before adding them to the slow cooker. Frozen items lower the temperatures in the cooker, affecting cook times and food safety.

RAISIN BREAD PUDDING

My sister gave me the recipe for this delicious bread pudding dotted with raisins. It's a big hit with everyone who's tried it. A homemade vanilla sauce comes together quickly on the stovetop and is drizzled over warm servings of this old-fashioned treat.

—SHERRY NIESE MCCOMB, OH

PREP: 20 MIN. • **COOK:** 4 HOURS • **MAKES:** 6 SERVINGS

- 8 **slices bread, cubed**
- 4 **large eggs**
- 2 **cups milk**
- ¼ **cup sugar**
- ¼ **cup butter, melted**
- ¼ **cup raisins**
- ½ **teaspoon ground cinnamon**

SAUCE

- 2 **tablespoons butter**
- 2 **tablespoons all-purpose flour**
- 1 **cup water**
- ¾ **cup sugar**
- 1 **teaspoon vanilla extract**

1. Place bread cubes in a greased 3-qt. slow cooker. In a large bowl, beat eggs and milk; stir in sugar, butter, raisins and cinnamon. Pour over bread; stir.

2. Cover and cook on high for 1 hour. Reduce heat to low; cook for 3-4 hours or until a thermometer reads 160°.

3. For sauce, melt butter in a small saucepan. Stir in flour until smooth. Gradually add water, sugar and vanilla. Bring to a boil; cook and stir for 2 minutes or until thickened. Serve with warm bread pudding.

HOT WING DIP

PREP: 10 MIN. • **COOK:** 1 HOUR
MAKES: 18 SERVINGS (¼ CUP EACH)

- 2 **cups shredded cooked chicken**
- 1 **package (8 ounces) cream cheese, cubed**
- 2 **cups shredded cheddar cheese**
- 1 **cup ranch salad dressing**
- ½ **cup Louisiana-style hot sauce**
  Tortilla chips and celery sticks
  Minced fresh parsley, optional

In a 3-qt. slow cooker, mix the first five ingredients. Cook, covered, on low for 1-2 hours or until the cheese is melted. Serve with chips and celery. If desired, sprinkle with parsley.

BAKED HOT WING DIP *Preheat oven to 350°. Spread dip mixture into an ungreased 9-in. square baking dish. Bake, uncovered, for 20-25 minutes or until heated through.*

Since I usually have all the ingredients on hand, this is a great go-to snack for entertaining friends and family.

—**COLEEN CORNER** GROVE CITY, PA

WARM CINNAMON PUNCH

Red Hot candies add rich color and spiciness to this festive punch, and the cranberry juice gives it a little tang.

—JULIE STERCHI CAMPBELLSVILLE, KY

PREP: 5 MIN. • **COOK:** 2 HOURS • **MAKES:** 8 SERVINGS (2 QUARTS)

- **1 bottle (32 ounces) cranberry juice**
- **5 cans (6 ounces each) unsweetened pineapple juice**
- **⅓ cup Red Hots**
- **1 cinnamon stick (3½ inches)**
  Additional cinnamon sticks, optional

1. In a 3-qt. slow cooker, combine juices, Red Hots and cinnamon stick. Cover and cook on low for 2-4 hours or until heated through and the candies are dissolved.
2. Discard the cinnamon stick before serving. Use additional cinnamon sticks as stirrers if desired.

NOTES

BACON CHEESE DIP

PREP: 15 MIN. • **COOK:** 2 HOURS • **MAKES:** 4 CUPS

- 2 **packages (8 ounces each) cream cheese, cubed**
- 4 **cups shredded cheddar cheese**
- 1 **cup half-and-half cream**
- 2 **teaspoons Worcestershire sauce**
- 1 **teaspoon dried minced onion**
- 1 **teaspoon prepared mustard**
- 16 **bacon strips, cooked and crumbled**
  Tortilla chips or French bread slices

1. In a 1½-qt. slow cooker, combine the first six ingredients. Cover and cook on low for 2-3 hours or until cheeses are melted, stirring occasionally.

2. Just before serving, stir in bacon. Serve warm with tortilla chips or bread.

BAKED BACON CHEESE DIP *Preheat oven to 375°. Transfer mixture to a 1-quart baking dish. Bake, uncovered, for 20-25 minutes or until bubbly.*

I've tried several appetizer recipes, but this one is a surefire people-pleaser. The thick dip has lots of bacon flavor and keeps friends happily munching.

—**SUZANNE WHITAKER** KNOXVILLE, TN

SWEET & TANGY CHICKEN WINGS

Here's a festive recipe that's perfect for parties. Put the wings in before you prepare for the party, and in a few hours you'll have wonderful appetizers!
—**IDA TUEY** SOUTH LYON, MI

PREP: 20 MIN. • **COOK:** 3¼ HOURS • **MAKES:** ABOUT 2½ DOZEN

- 3 **pounds chicken wingettes (about 30)**
- ½ **teaspoon salt, divided**
- **Dash pepper**
- 1½ **cups ketchup**
- ¼ **cup packed brown sugar**
- ¼ **cup red wine vinegar**
- 2 **tablespoons Worcestershire sauce**
- 1 **tablespoon Dijon mustard**
- 1 **teaspoon minced garlic**
- 1 **teaspoon liquid smoke, optional**
- **Sesame seeds, optional**

1. Sprinkle chicken with a dash of salt and pepper. Broil 4-6 in. from the heat for 5-10 minutes on each side or until golden brown. Transfer to a greased 5-qt. slow cooker.

2. Combine ketchup, brown sugar, vinegar, Worcestershire sauce, mustard, garlic, liquid smoke (if desired) and the remaining salt; pour over the wings. Toss to coat.

3. Cover and cook on low for 3¼-3¾ hours or until chicken juices run clear. Sprinkle with sesame seeds if desired.

FREEZE OPTION *Freeze cooled fully-cooked wings in freezer containers. To use, partially thaw in refrigerator overnight. Reheat wings in a foil-lined 15x10x1-in. baking pan in a preheated 325° oven until heated through, covering if necessary to prevent browning. Serve as directed.*

SLOW COOKER CIDER

PREP: 5 MIN. • **COOK:** 2 HOURS
MAKES: 2 QUARTS

- 2 **cinnamon sticks (3 inches)**
- 1 **teaspoon whole cloves**
- 1 **teaspoon whole allspice**
- 2 **quarts apple cider**
- ½ **cup packed brown sugar**
- 1 **orange, sliced**

1. Place cinnamon, cloves and allspice on a double thickness of cheesecloth; bring up corners of cloth and tie with a string to form a bag.

2. Place cider and brown sugar in a 3-qt. slow cooker; stir until sugar dissolves. Add spice bag. Place orange slices on top. Cover and cook on low for 2-3 hours or until heated through. Discard spice bag.

There's no last-minute rush when you slowly simmer this punch.

—**ALPHA WILSON** ROSWELL, NM

CRAB & ARTICHOKE DIP

Whenever my girlfriends and I get together, someone brings this rich and creamy dip and someone else brings our favorite bottle of wine. Because the recipe relies on slow cooker convenience, it's a smart choice for busy people.

—**CONNIE MCKINNEY** MARSHALL, MO

PREP: 20 MIN. • **COOK:** 2 HOURS • **MAKES:** 3½ CUPS

- 3 **cups fresh baby spinach**
- 1 **can (14 ounces) water-packed artichoke hearts, rinsed, drained and chopped**
- 1 **package (8 ounces) cream cheese, softened**
- 2 **cups shredded Havarti cheese**
- 1 **can (6 ounces) lump crabmeat, drained**
- ½ **cup sour cream**
- ⅛ **teaspoon salt**
- ⅛ **teaspoon pepper**
  Assorted crackers

1. In a large saucepan, bring ½ in. of water to a boil. Add spinach; cover and boil for 3-5 minutes or until wilted. Drain.
2. In a 1½-qt. slow cooker, combine the artichokes, cheeses, crabmeat, sour cream, salt, pepper and spinach. Cover and cook on low for 2-3 hours or until cheeses are melted. Serve with crackers.

NOTES

MOLTEN MOCHA CAKE

PREP: 10 MIN. • **COOK:** 2½ HOURS • **MAKES:** 4 SERVINGS

- 4 **large eggs**
- 1½ **cups sugar**
- ½ **cup butter, melted**
- 3 **teaspoons vanilla extract**
- 1 **cup all-purpose flour**
- ½ **cup baking cocoa**
- 1 **tablespoon instant coffee granules**
- ¼ **teaspoon salt**
  Fresh raspberries or sliced fresh strawberries and vanilla ice cream, optional

1. In a large bowl, beat eggs, sugar, butter and vanilla until blended. In another bowl, whisk flour, cocoa, coffee granules and salt; gradually beat into egg mixture.

2. Transfer to greased 1½-qt. slow cooker. Cook, covered, on low 2½-3 hours or until a toothpick comes out with moist crumbs. If desired, serve warm cake with berries and ice cream.

My daughter says this cake is one of her favorite desserts. I once shared the cake with my neighbor's son. He liked it so much that he ate the whole thing without telling anyone about it!

—**AIMEE FORTNEY** FAIRVIEW, TN

BARBECUE MEATBALLS

I whipped these up for my son's first birthday so I could serve something heartier alongside the cake and ice cream. They're delicious!
—**TARA REEDER** MASON, MI

PREP: 20 MIN. • **COOK:** 7 HOURS
MAKES: 2 DOZEN

- 1 **large egg, beaten**
- ½ **cup shredded Colby-Monterey Jack cheese**
- ¼ **cup seasoned bread crumbs**
- ¼ **cup finely chopped onion**
- 2 **pounds ground beef**

SAUCE

- 2 **cups ketchup**
- 2 **tablespoons prepared mustard**
- 1 **tablespoon brown sugar**
- 1 **tablespoon cider vinegar**
- 1 **tablespoon lemon juice**
- 1 **tablespoon soy sauce**

1. In a large bowl, combine the egg, cheese, bread crumbs and onion. Crumble beef over mixture and mix well. Shape into 1½-in. balls. Transfer to a 3-qt. slow cooker.

2. In a small bowl, combine the sauce ingredients; pour over meatballs. Cover and cook on low for 7-8 hours or until meat is no longer pink.

GENERAL INDEX

ALPHABETICAL INDEX